THE 'AQĪDAH OF IMĀM
AN-NAWAWĪ

The 'Aqidah of Imam an-Nawawi

1st Edition © Jamiah Media 2010 C.E. / 1431 A.H.

ISBN: 978-0-9551099-8-0

Published by:

Published by Jamiah Media
Email: admin@salafimanhaj.com

Source of translation: Extract from Shaykh Mashhūr's Saheeh Muslim class dated Thursday 20 April 2006 CE. (www.mashhoor.net)

Cover design & Typesetting: Ihsaan Design - www.ihsaandesign.co.uk

THE 'AQĪDAH OF IMĀM
AN-NAWAWĪ

ABU ZAKARIYYAH YAHYA BIN SHARAF AN-NAWAWI ﷺ
(D,767 A.H.)

BY THE NOBLE SHAYKH

MASHHŪR HASAN ĀL SALMĀN حفظه الله

Translated by 'AbdulHaq ibn Kofi ibn Kwesi al-Ashanti

With additional work by Azhar Abu Faatimah and Amr Abualrub

Contents

Translator's Preface

Indeed, all praise is due to Allāh, we praise Him, we seek His aid, and we ask for His forgiveness. We seek refuge in Allāh from the evil of our actions and from the evil consequences of our actions. Whomever Allāh guides, there is none to misguide and whoever Allāh misguides there is none to guide. I bear witness that there is no god worthy of worship except Allāh and I bear witness that Muhammad is the servant and Messenger of Allāh.

﴿ يَـٰٓأَيُّهَا ٱلَّذِينَ ءَامَنُوا۟ ٱتَّقُوا۟ ٱللَّهَ حَقَّ تُقَاتِهِۦ وَلَا تَمُوتُنَّ إِلَّا وَأَنتُم مُّسْلِمُونَ ﴾

"O you who have believed, fear Allāh as He should be feared and do not die except as Muslims (in submission to Him)." *{Āli-Imrān (3): 102}*

﴿ يَـٰٓأَيُّهَا ٱلنَّاسُ ٱتَّقُوا۟ رَبَّكُمُ ٱلَّذِى خَلَقَكُم مِّن نَّفْسٍ وَٰحِدَةٍ وَخَلَقَ مِنْهَا زَوْجَهَا وَبَثَّ مِنْهُمَا رِجَالًا كَثِيرًا وَنِسَآءً ۚ وَٱتَّقُوا۟ ٱللَّهَ ٱلَّذِى تَسَآءَلُونَ بِهِۦ وَٱلْأَرْحَامَ ۚ إِنَّ ٱللَّهَ كَانَ عَلَيْكُمْ رَقِيبًا ﴾

"O mankind, fear your Lord, who created you from one soul and created from it its mate and dispersed from both of them many men and women. And fear Allāh through whom you ask things from each other, and

(respect) the wombs. Indeed Allāh is ever, over you, an Observer." *{an-Nisā (4): 1}*

﴿ يَٰٓأَيُّهَا ٱلَّذِينَ ءَامَنُوا۟ ٱتَّقُوا۟ ٱللَّهَ وَقُولُوا۟ قَوْلًا سَدِيدًا. يُصْلِحْ لَكُمْ أَعْمَٰلَكُمْ وَيَغْفِرْ لَكُمْ ذُنُوبَكُمْ ۗ وَمَن يُطِعِ ٱللَّهَ وَرَسُولَهُۥ فَقَدْ فَازَ فَوْزًا عَظِيمًا ﴾

"O you who have believed, fear Allāh and speak words of appropriate justice. He will amend for you your deeds and forgive your sins. And whoever obeys Allāh and His Messenger has certainly attained a great attainment." *{al-Ahzāb (33): 70-71}*

To proceed: This is a translation of an outstanding work by our respected Shaykh from Jordan, the Usūlī and Faqeeh on the *manhaj* of *Ahl ul-Hadīth*, Mashhūr bin Hasan Āl Salmān, may Allāh preserve him. This work will look at an issue which has been contentious for some which is ascertaining the creed of the great Imām, Abū Zakariyā Yahyā an-Nawawī ﷺ. It will be evident within this translation that the Ashā'irah, who claim that Imām an-Nawawī was absolutely Ash'ari, are particularly unconvincing in terms of 'aqeedah and thus their arguments have been found wanting. This is due to a number of reasons which can be summed up with the following:

- The neutrality deficit within much contemporary Ash'ari writing, to the extent that their writing assumes a polemical standing as opposed to a critical academic survey of ascertaining the correct 'aqeedah. Shaykh Faisal al-Jāsim demonstrates in his work *al-Ash'ār'irah fī Mīzān Ahl is-Sunnah* [The 'Ash'arīs in the Scales of Ahl us-Sunnah] for example, that in many cases the

two Ashʿarī authors who he critiques throughout his book[1] totally neglect any referral to certain extant creedal works and continue as if nothing has even been written. This kind of approach seems to maintain partisan loyalties and is far from academic impartiality.

- The adamant Ashʿarī assertion, which serves as more of an *argumentum ad nauseam,* that Salafīs are anthropomorphists. It is plain from the works which Salafīs utilise in *ʿaqeedah* that nothing of the sort is found therein, rather there are abundant rejections of *tamtheel, tajseem* and *tasbheeh,* as there are refutations of *taʿteel, taʾweel* and *tafweedh (of the meaning).*

- The Ashʿarī agreement with the Muʿtazilah in many of their interpretations of the texts and their agreement with them regarding Allāh's Speech not being comprised of letters and sounds.

- The Ashʿarī agreement with the Jahmiyyah in regards to Allāh's Attributes, this agreement with them is exemplified in the writings of Zāhid al-Kawtharī, who even defended Jahm bin Safwān! His excessive statements and even *takfeer* of scholars will be studied in a future paper.

- The contemporary Ashʿarī claim of a "*Salafī conspiracy to tamper with classical texts*" in order to further Salafiyyah. This preposterous assertion is probably the epitome of such contemporary Ashʿarī intellectual bankruptcy and polemic. So after it is demonstrated that the ʿAshaʾrīs have a contrary approach to *ʿaqeedah* in light of the Qurʾān, Sunnah, *Ijmā* of the

---

[1] Faisal bin Qazār al-Jāsim, *al-Ashaʾirah fī Mīzān Ahl us-Sunnah: Naqd li-Kitāb Ahl us-Sunnati al-ʾAshaʾiratu: Shahādatu ʾUlama il-Ummati wa Adilatuhum* [The Ashʿarīs in the Scales of the People of Sunnah: A Critique of the Book 'The Ashʿarīs are *Ahl us-Sunnah*: The Testimony of the Scholars of the Ummah and their Evidences']. Kuwait: al-Mabarah al-Khayriyyah li Ulūm il-Qurʾan waʾs-Sunnah, 1428 AH/2007 CE. The book has been translated and will be published soon *inshāʾAllāh.*

Salaf and creeds of the Imāms of the early generations – the final evasion becomes: "Actually, we don't trust your sources, they have been tampered with!" Nūh Keller, who has written a variety of rather obscurantist and polemical articles, even attempted to demonstrate this in a rather haphazard attempt to prove their contention.[2] Yet it is apparent that to claim that there has been an intentional *"Salafī conspiracy to tamper with texts"* would mean that somehow the Salafīs (from the 19th century or 1980s – according to their non-concurring dates of when Salafiyyah became popularised) would had to have had access to a vast range of manuscripts, collections and folios to tamper with, and this is obviously implausible.

One latest example of this inadequate comprehension of 'aqeedah is the fact that only recently have some Western Ash'arī teachers admitted that there is such a thing as the "Salafī" or "Atharī" 'aqeedah, even though this has been emphasised in the West for the last fifteen years. Indeed, it

---

[2] As can be seen in an article written in the mid 1990s entitled *Reforming Classical Texts* by Mas'ūd Khān from Aylesbury, which was a question put to his teacher, Nūh Keller. Such a question would be of little benefit to Khān who cannot access the classical texts in the original Arabic language in any case, so it would be perhaps better to actually study Arabic first before accusing Salafīs of the very serious crime of tampering with and purposefully covering up what is found within books which may oppose them.

Just one example which indicates that this is incorrect is that fact that writings and manuscripts of books of those who wrote against Imām Muhammad ibn 'AbdulWahhāb are still extant to this day within Saudi libraries. The works of Ahmad bin 'Ali ash-Shāfi'ī al-Qabbānī for example are to be found in the library of Imām Muhammad ibn Saud University in Riyadh. This demonstrates that the opposing arguments have been preserved in order to rebut them and shows that the followers of Imām Muhammad ibn 'AbdulWahhāb did not totally destroy, desecrate and ransack the works, writings and books of their opponents. Qabbānī had two writings against Muhammad ibn 'AbdulWahhāb, the first was a copy in his handwriting of a book entitled *Kitāb Rad ad-Dalālah wa Qama' al-Jahālah* by another scholar called Ahmad Barakat ash-Shāfi'ī al-Azharī at-Tandatāwī. While the second is entitled *Kitāb Naqd Qawā'id ad-Dalāl wa Rafd 'Aqā'id ud-Dullāl* which is a response to a letter sent by Imām Muhammad ibn 'AbdulWahhāb to the 'Ulamā in Basra.

seems that this recognition of the Salafī 'aqeedah has more to do with the current ecumenical zeitgeist among some Muslims as a front for "unity", in light of recent events affecting Muslim communities in the West, more than it has to do with a serious critical evidence-based investigation of the correct 'aqeedah as documented from the Salaf. The dearth of evidences is just one issue which causes many to disregard the Asharite creed and its speculative-rhetorical approach. Of late however, for a variety of reasons, there has been an increase in Ash'arī polemic and its dialectic is resurfacing. Leading the way in this regard have been the following Ash'arī apologists who have authored and translated a variety of polemical tracts:

- G.F Haddād – the "*Mureed*" of Hishām al-Kabbānī (the deputy of Nazim Qubrusī, head of an eccentric trend of the Naqshbandī Sūfī cult).[3] Kabbānī can be witnessed here performing a "dance".[4]
- 'Abdullāh bin Hamīd 'Ali – a proponent of a polemical variety of Mālikī fiqh parochialism. Originally hailing from Philadelphia, he has recently assumed a teaching position with the Zaytuna Institute in Santa Clara, California.
- TJ Winter (Abdul-Hakīm Murād) – a Cambridge University Professor of Divinity Theology.
- Abū Layth ash-Shāfiʿī[5]
- Abū Jaʿfar al-Misrī al-Hanbalī[6]

---

[3] Interestingly, other strands of *Naqshbandiyyah* make *takfeer* of Nazim Qubrusī! Not even *tabdiʾ* or *tadleel* but *takfeer*! As occurred from Sameer al-Kādī ar-Rifāʿī, another Naqshabandī leader who is vying with Nazim for control of the cult.

[4] See:
http://video.google.co.uk/videoplay?docid=618545744089582463&q=Kabbani+sufi+dhikr
http://uk.youtube.com/watch?v=r_YYpDRknjU&feature=related
http://uk.youtube.com/watch?v=ncQi1FGYL9U&feature=related

[5] http://seekingilm.com/

[6] http://www.htspub.com/

- The Marifah.net website[7] - their work, which remains largely polemical, attempts to present the Ash'arī creed in a more academic and sophisticated manner, yet the arguments presented are still inconclusive in aiding the Ash'arī creedal position. And others.

Much of the writing of the above however has demonstrated a distinct lack of academic impartiality not to mention falling short in terms of intellectual consistency. The lack of academic neutrality which has led to such intellectual bankruptcy and ahistoricity on the part of some contemporary Ash'arīs is inadequate, especially considering the fact that they are deemed by some quarters as representing a "scholarly" tradition. Manifestly however, when it comes to writing about the Salafīs and issues related to creed, impartiality and objectivity, which are the hallmarks of professional academic writing, totally go out of the window. This rather haphazard and unsophisticated approach is a form of cognitive bias, resulting from intellectual bias and partisanship.[8] It is also a form of intellectual denial on the part of the contemporary Ash'arīs and Māturīdīs. Take for example a recent remark made by TJ Winter (Abdul-Hakīm Murād) in the introduction to the *Cambridge Companion to Classical Islamic Theology* (Cambridge: Cambridge University Press, 2008), p.10[9]:

---

[7] www.marifah.net

[8] One example of this can be seen in a question posed to Nūh Keller in the mid 1990s by Mas'ud Khan of Aylesbury; the question was entitled '*Was Imām Ahmad an anthropomorphist as claimed by the Salafis?*' Yet it is evident that this is an excellent example of a Straw man argument. Khan exaggerates and distorts (and that's putting it mildly!) the Salafi position and puts words into the Salafis' mouths claiming that they've forwarded an argument which they haven't actually made. Furthermore, within the answer Keller claims that *Kitāb us-Sunnah* is falsely ascribed to 'Abdullāh bin Ahmad bin Hanbal yet provides no evidence whatsoever, this is not adequate for serious scholarship and research.

[9] It can be referred to here:
http://assets.cambridge.org/97805217/85495/excerpt/9780521785495_excerpt.pdf

Certainly, it is intriguing that the Hanbalī alternative in most places represented no more than a small fringe, just as the Hanbalī definition of Sharī'a remained the smallest of the rites of law. The iconic hard-line champion of this school, Ibn Taymiyya…is not conspicuous in the catalogues of Islamic manuscript libraries; his current renown is a recent phenomenon. Ibn Taymiyya was, indeed, imprisoned for heresy, a relatively unusual occurrence, and it would be hard to imagine Muslim society, or its rulers or scholars, punishing more philosophical thinkers like Ghazālī, or Razī, or Taftāzānī, in the same way. 'Hard' Hanbalism offered a simple literalism to troubled urban masses, and occasionally won their violent, riotous support, but the consensus of Muslims passed it by.

An exquisite illustration of such contemporary Ash'arī academic obscurantism littered with selective perception and then topped off with a dash of polemical exuberance to boot! Let's deconstruct this intellectual irregularity and ahistorical reading of events:

Firstly, the suggestion that Ibn Taymiyyah "is not conspicuous in the catalogues of Islamic manuscript libraries" and that "his current renown is a recent phenomenon" is absolutely incorrect. Muslim academics and specialists such as Dr Muhammad 'Uzayr Shams in his work *al-Jāmi' li's-Sirat Shaykh ul-Islām Ibn Taymiyyah Khilāl Sab'at Qurūn* (Makkah, KSA: Dār 'Ālam ul-Fawā'id, 1422 AH) and even non-Muslim academics such as Professor Caterina Bori, have adequately demonstrated that Ibn Taymiyyah is indeed conspicuous within the manuscripts. Bori states in her paper *The Collection and Edition of Ibn Taymiyyah's Works: Concerns of a Disciple*:

> With this in mind, the role of his circle of pupils must have been crucial in the process of transmission of his work. The massive 37-volume fatwa collection of Ibn

Taymīyah, the many printed books of his writings available on the market today, and the large number of manuscripts lying scattered in libraries all over the world encourage one to imagine a steady, ongoing, and successful transmission throughout the centuries.

Dr Bori then states:

> An impressive amount of biographical material on Ibn Taymīyah has survived. No other contemporary scholar was the subject of such a large number of biographical writings. Among these, two monographs written shortly after his death stand out, together with a third, later one, which does not impress the reader with its originality—in fact, it draws heavily on previous materials. A series of biographical entries in collective dictionaries or obituaries in chronicles adds to this bulk of texts. To my knowledge, no other fourteenth-century scholar was inundated by such a cascade of bio-hagiographical attention, let alone the single-subject volumes composed for him in the style of manāqib (usually monographic biographical works of a laudatory nature).[10]

These observations rebut the assertion that Ibn Taymiyyah "is not conspicuous in the catalogues of Islamic manuscript libraries" and that "his current renown is a recent phenomenon". Bori notes that Ibn Taymiyyah's works were recovered after his death by the Amīr Sayfuddeen Qutlūbughā al-Fakhrī (d. 742 AH/1343 CE) while Ibn Murrī, al-Mizzī (d. 742 AH/1341-42 CE), Ibn Rushayyiq (749 AH/1348 CE), Ibn Katheer (d. 774AH/1373 CE), Ibn 'AbdulHādī and Ibn ul-Qayyim were all important in preserving the works of Ibn Taymiyyah due to the large body of works available. Ibn Rushayyiq, a

---

[10] Caterina Bori, "*The Collection and Edition of Ibn Taymiyyah's Works: Concerns of a Disciple*" in Mamlūk Studies Review, vol.8, no.2 (July 2009), p.51.

Mālikī and faithful student of Ibn Taymiyyah was the one who was most dedicated to the collection and edition of his works.[11]

Secondly, the claim that Ibn Taymiyyah was "punished" by the Muslim society of his time is also a shocking suggestion from Winter. Not only is it well known from the sources that Ibn Taymiyyah was loved by the Damascene populace, but Ibn Taymiyyah also had superb relations with the rulers of his time as we can see with the following examples:

- Bori highlights that Biographical sources and chronicles report plenty of evidence regarding the evidence regarding the relationship between Ibn Taymiyyah and the Mamlūk authorities. For example, Ibn Taymiyyah had good relations with the Amīr Sayfuddeen Jāghān the finance agent *(Mushidd ud-Dawāween)* in Damascus between 697-702/1297-1303 who was also the deputy of the viceroy.

- Ibn Taymiyyah also had good relations with the governor of Damascus Jamāluddeen al-Afram (d.720 AH/1320-21 CE) and Ibn Katheer reports in *al-Bidāyah wa'n-Nihāyah* that Ibn Taymiyyah accompanied him one some military campaigns.

- Ibn Taymiyyah's role between the Mongol and Egyptian authorities is also recorded in several chronicles such as al-Birzālī (d. 739 AH/1339 CE); Ibn Katheer in *al-Bidāyah wa'n-Nihāyah*, vol.14, p.8, 14; al-Yūnīnī (d. 726 AH/1326 CE) in his *Dhayl Mir'āt uz-Zamān*, vol.2, pp.108-109, 119, 123-24 (ed. Li Guo, Leiden, 1998); Ibn Dawādārī (d. 736 AH/1335 CE) in his *Kanz ad-Durar wa Jāmi' al-Ghurar*, vol.9, pp.32-33, 36 (ed. Hans Robert Roemer, Cairo, 1960) and an-Nuwayrī (d. 733 AH/1333 CE) in *Nihāyat ul-'Arab fī Funūn il-Adab*, vol.31, p.395 (ed. Al-Bāz al-'Arīnī, Cairo, 1992).

---

[11] Ibid., p.57

- Ibn 'AbdulHādī reports in *al-'Uqūd*, pp.282-293 that Sultān Qalawūn (d. 741 AH/1341 CE) after regaining power in 709 AH/1310 CE asked Ibn Taymiyyah to avenge his enemies with a fatwa but Ibn Taymiyyah refused this offer.

Thirdly, what Winter has done here is to regurgitate what Dr Yahya Michot, currently Professor of Islamic Studies at the Hartford Seminary, calls the "Ibn Taymiyyah myth" which seeks to portray Ibn Taymiyyah as some sort of "big baddie" who is responsible for all things negative within the Muslim world today. There is no doubt that such an assessment is simplistic and, as Dr Yahya Michot has stated, is also too general to claim that Ibn Taymiyyah is not "conspicuous in the catalogues of Islamic manuscript libraries" as there has not been a detailed corpus of Ibn Taymiyyah's works compiled based on the manuscripts around the world, let alone a thorough survey of where Ibn Taymiyyah has been highlighted within the manuscripts.[12]

Fourthly, historically it was the other way round! Murād (Winter) in his writings neatly skips over any referral whatsoever of how the Ash'arī speculative theological system came to the fore. In fact, the Ash'arīs were

---

[12] I had the opportunity to ask Dr Yahya Michot this question on Friday 18th July 2008 at a lecture on Ibn Taymiyyah held at London's City Circle. Dr Yahya is currently regarded as the main Western specialist in the works of Shaykh ul-Islām Ibn Taymiyyah and has written a wealth of material on him largely in French. He does have four works in English one which has been published and the other three are due for publication later in 2008. His book *Muslims under non-Muslim Rule: Ibn Taymiyya on fleeing from sin, kinds of emigration and the status of Mardin* (Oxford and London: Interface Publications, 2006) is a translation and study of Ibn Taymiyyah's *fatwa* on Mardin and Dr Yahya corroborates exactly as Shaykh, Dr Khālid al-Anbarī did in his book *The Impact of Man-Made Laws* and in the audio lectures *Politics in Light of Islām* (which can be downloaded from salafimanhaj.com). Dr Yahya has also conducted research detailing how many of the modern-day takfeerīs have totally mis-read and misused Ibn Taymiyyah's fatāwā in that they have taken Ibn Taymiyyah's fatāwā regarding the Mongols and applied them to the rulers of the Muslim lands, again corroborating what the Salafi scholars have highlighted for years. Dr Yahya currently teaches classical Arabic and Islamic theology at Oxford University and is due to hold a position at the Hartford Seminary in America.

rebuked for their views before they attained dominance and were regarded as a heretical fringe fraternity. MacDonald also notes, in following Ibn Taymiyyah, adh-Dhahabī and Ibn ul-Mabrad, that the Ash'arīs were rebuked "from the pulpits of mosques"[13] and that many Ash'arīs fled Baghdād and Persia as a result. For the Ash'arī creed only gained dominance after the Abbasid minister Nidhām al-Mulk came into power and established institutions (*Nidhāmiyyah*) wherein the Asharite speculative-rhetorical creed could be instructed, al-Ghazālī at one point was the head of the institution.[14] Hye states:

> **Nizam al-Mulk founded the Nizamite Academy in Baghdad in 459 AH/1066 CE for the defence of Asharite doctrines. It is under his patronage that Abu al-Ma'ali 'Abd al-Malik al-Juwaini got the chance of preaching the Ash'arite doctrine freely.**[15]

So in the year when William the Conqueror and his Norman armies took control of England suppressing the Anglo-Saxon English, Nidhām ul-Mulk and the Ash'arīs were taking control of Islamic educational institutions in the Muslim state and suppressing the Hanbalīs. Surely Winter should be aware of this? Such a denial and lack of referral to this historical event by the contemporary Ash'arīs is but one example of their intellectual denial. The Abbasid support of Ibn al-Qushayrī, an Asharite rhetorician, led to disturbances within Baghdād with the majority of the Hanbalī orientated public rejecting the newly fangled Ash'arī creedal system. This event has been referred to in Islamic history as the *Fitnah Qushayriyyah* and at this point the Hanbalīs were suppressed by the state which had succumbed to 'Ash'arite creedal dialectic. Ibn Katheer

---

[13] D.B. MacDonald, *Development of Muslim Theology, Jurisprudence and Constitutional Theory* (London: George Routledge and Sons, 1903), p.212. There will be more mentioned about this in detail within the last chapter of this translation.

[14] M.H. Zuberi, *Aristotle and Al-Ghazali* (Delhi, India: Noor Publishing House, 1992), pp.29-30

[15] M.A. Hye (2004), *"Asharism"* in M.M. Sharif (ed.), *A History of Muslim Philosophy* (Wiesbaden, Germany: Otto Harrassowitz, 1963-6), vol.1, p.242

mentions this event in *al-Bidāyah wa'n-Nihāyah* and states that Ibn al-Qushayrī, along with some others, wrote to Nidhām ul-Mulk accusing the Hanābilah of *tajseem* (anthropomorphism) and other things. This caused a commotion which led to a mob of Asharites physically attacking one of the Hanbalī Shaykhs, Shareef Abū Ja'far bin Abī Mūsā, at his masjid wherein one was killed and others injured. Not to mention the fact that al-Juwaynī and Nidhām ul-Mulk were close friends and reciprocates in religio-political outlook[16], so does this sound familiar? Indeed, Ibn 'Asākir in his *Tabyeen Kadhib al-Muftarī*, who was writing at the height of the Ash'arī inquisition (in the sixth Islamic century) never at all in his writings claimed that the Ash'arīs were the majority as the contemporary Ash'arīs try to use as a proof. Rather, he merely argued that the arguments were correct yet accepted that they were a minority. Note that Ibn 'Asākir was writing in refutation of al-Ahwāzī who argued that the Ash'arīs were a newly fangled fringe group which had heretical beliefs. The famous Muslim historian al-Maqrīzī stated in his monumental work *Khutat*:

> The madhdhab of Abu'l-Hasan al-Ash'arī spread in 'Irāq from around 380 AH and from there spread to Shām (the Levant). When the victorious king Salāhuddeen Yūsuf bin Ayyūb (Saladin) took control over Egypt, his main judge Sadruddeen 'AbdulMalik bin 'Īsā bin Darbās al-Mārānī and himself were adherents to this school of thought. The madhdhab was also spread by the just ruler Nūruddeen Mahmood bin Zinkī in Damascus. Salāhuddeen memorised a text authored by Qutbuddeen Abu'l-Ma'ālī Mas'ood bin Muhammad bin Mas'ūd an-Naysabūrī and this (Ash'arī) text was then studied and memorised by Salāhuddeen's offspring. This gave prominence and status to the madhdhab (attributed) to al-Ash'arī and

---

[16] M.R. Hassan (2004), *"Nizam al-Mulk Tusi"* in MM Sharif (ed.), op.cit., pp.747-774

was taken on board by the people during their rule.[17] This was continued by all of the successive rulers from Banī Ayyūb (the Ayyubids) and then during the rule of the Turkish kings (Mamluks).

Abū 'Abdullāh Muhammad bin Tumart, one of the rulers of al-Maghrib (Morocco), agreed with this (Ash'arī) trend when he travelled to al-'Irāq. He took the Ash'arī madhdhab on board via Abū Hāmid al-Ghazālī and when Ibn Tumart returned to al-Maghrib he caused a clash[18] and began to teach the people of the land the Ash'arī madhdhab and instituted it for the people. When he died 'AbdulMumin bin 'Alī al-Mīsī succeeded him and was referred to as the 'leader of the believers', him and his sons seized control of Morocco and were named the "Muwahhiddūn" ('the monotheists'). This is how the Muwahhidūn state came to fruition in Morocco and they shed the blood of all who opposed the 'aqeedah laid down by Ibn Tumart, who they viewed as being the infallible Mahdī.[19] Look how many were killed during that the numbers of which can only be enumerated by Allāh ﷻ, this is well known within the history books.

---

[17] Furthermore, the Ash'arīs in Egypt during that time were active against the Fatimiyyah Rawāfid who were ruling over Egypt, as a result the institution of a formal creed was a move to quell the development of the Rawāfid within Egypt and Shām. The Fatimid-Shi'a built al-Azhar University and when Salāhuddeen defeated the Fatimids their teachings were replaced with what the Ash'arīs there had codified.

[18] Ibn Tumart, after debating with the scholars of Fez, was deemed to be a radical and was thus imprisoned for his beliefs and views at the bequest of the *Murābit* (Almoravid) ruler at the time 'Ali bin Yūsuf.

[19] Ibn Tumart actually declared himself to be a descendent of the Prophet ﷺ and the Mahdī while he was promoting the Asharite creed in Morocco and North Africa and rebelling against the *Murabitoon* Muslim leaders!

This was the reason for the spread of the madhdhab (attributed to) al-Ash'arī and how it spread within the Islamic lands. This is to the extent that all other madhāhib (of Sunnī 'aqeedah) have been forgotten and people are ignorant of if to the extent that today there exists no other madhdhab (of Sunnī 'aqeedah) contrary to it! Except for the madhdhab of the Hanbalīs who follow Imām Abū 'Abdullāh Ahmad bin Muhammad bin Hanbal ﷺ, for they were upon the way of the Salaf and did not view that any form of figurative interpretation be made about Allāh's Attributes. So after seven hundred years after the Hijrah the actions of the Hanbalīs became famed in Damascus due to Taqīuddeen Abu'l-'Abbās Ahmad bin 'AbdulHakam bin 'AbdusSalām bin Taymiyyah al-Harrānī. He supported the madhdhab of the Salaf and exerted great efforts in refuting the madhdhab of the Asha'irah and he strongly criticised them as well as the Rāfidah and Sūfiyyah.[20]

Fifthly, the "rites of law" (i.e. *madhāhib*) and their spread, was due to power and politics as is evident from even a brief historical survey. The idea that the *madhāhib* were spread around the Islamic world by a mere "unbroken chain of transmission" that was "handed down traditionally" is a romantic ahistorical reading of events. For example, al-Maqrīzī in *Khutat Misr* notes:

> The people of Ifreeqiyyah (Africa) mostly used to follow the Sunnah and the Āthār. Then the Hanafī madhhab took over and then after that, the Mālikī madhhab; the latter ones following earlier ones in the playing of the companions of desires and self-interest.

---

[20] Al-Maqrīzī, al-Khutat: *al-Mawā'idh wa'l-I'tibār bi Dhikr il-Khutat wa'l-Athār* (Cairo: Maktabah ath-Thaqafiyyah ad-Deeniyyah, n.d.), vol.4, p.192

All the people of the nations which the companions conquered used to be described with the name '*Ahl ul-Hadeeth*', as Abū Mansoor 'AbdulQādir ibn Tāhir at-Tamīmī al-Baghdādī said in his book *Usool ud-Deen* (vol.1, p.317):

It is clear that the people of the lands of ar-Rūm (Byzantium), al-Jazeerah (the Arabian Peninsula), ash-Shām (the Levant), Adharbayjān (Azerbaijan), Bāb ul-Abwāb (Darband/Derbent)[21] and others which were conquered were all upon the madhhab of the Ahl ul-Hadeeth. Also the inhabitants of the lands of Ifreeqiyyah (Africa), Andalus (Andalusia) and all the countries behind the Western Sea, were from the Ahl ul-Hadeeth. Also the people of the lands of al-Yaman

---

[21] Or 'Derbend', written and pronounced as 'Derbent' in Russian, it is a town in Daghestan on the Western shore of the Caspian Sea that was known to the Arabs. See Houtsma, Van Donzel (eds.) E.J. Brill's First Encyclopaedia of Islam: 1913-1936 (Leiden, Netherlands: EJ Brill: 1993), p.940. Derbent is the southernmost city in Russia which is thought to be the oldest city in the whole of Russia. Derbend was known as the 'Caspian Gates' in the West and Bāb ul-Abwāb ('The Gate of Gates') in the Arabic-speaking Islamic world, but its name has always been linked to 'gates' of a fortress. The name "The Gate of Gates" originates in the fact that Derbend consisted of thirty north-facing towers which stretched for 40 kilometres between the Caspian Sea and the Caucasus Mountains. The immense wall had a height of up to twenty meters and a thickness of about 10 feet (3 m) when it was in use. It was built by Yazdegird, the Second of the Sassanid-Persian Empire (in circa 440 CE) and was attacked by the Armenians and Albanians in their rebellion in 450 CE. Kisra the First strengthened it during his reign (531-579) in order to keep out the Gokturks. Some historians have confused the fortress walls with the Gates of Alexander which he built as a barrier in the Caucasus to prevent the non-Greeks of the north attacking the south. Some historians still maintain that the fortress built by Kisra may have had earlier foundations built by the Achaemenid Persian Empire (550–330 BCE), these were later conquered by the Greeks so the fortress may have been reinforced by agents of Alexander's empire. Darband (Derbent) is not to be confused with the four other towns today that have the name 'Darband'. One town/district in Tajikistan; a village next to Tehrān in Irān; a town in Western Baluchistan and the other a village in the Mansehra District in North-Western Pakistan.

(Yemen) upon the Zanj coastline (Zanzibar) were all from the Ahl ul-Hadeeth.[22]

Al-Maqrīzī also notes in *al-Khutat* (vol.3, p.333):

Most of Ifreeqiyyah (Africa) was upon the Sunnah and Āthār, until 'Abdullāh ibn Farrookh Abū Muhammad al-Fārisi came with the Hanafī madhhab, then Asad ibn al-Furāt ibn Senān became the judge of Ifreeqiyyah, upon the Hanafī madhhab. When Sahnoon ibn Sa'eed at-Tanūkhī took judgeship of Ifreeqiyyah, the Mālikī madhhab spread amongst them. Then al-Mu'izz ibn Bādees made all of the people of Ifreeqiyyah adhere to the Mālikī madhhab and leave everything else. So the people of Ifreeqiyyah (Africa) and the people of al-Andalus (Andalusia) were turned to the Mālikī madhhab right up until today, due to the desire of the rulers and their desire for the world. So the judgements and rulings in all those towns and villages were not given except by one who had ascribed themselves to the fiqh of the Mālikī madhhab...

This is also mentioned by the historians Ibn ul-Atheer in *al-Kāmil fi't-Tāreekh* and Ibn Khallikān in *Mawāsim ul-Ādāb*. Ibn Hajar mentions in *Raf' ul-Isr*, as does as-Sakhāwī in *ath-Thighar al-Bassām* that:

Ibn 'Uthmān ad-Dimishqī al-Qādī was the first one to bring the Shāfi'ī madhhab into ash-Shām and he took over the judgeship of Dimashq (Damascus), ruling by it. He was followed by those who succeeded him and he used to give a reward of 100 deenārs to the ones who memorised Mukhtasar ul-Muzanī.

In *Tabaqāt as-Subkī, al-I'lān wa't-Tawbeekh* and *Shadharāt adh-Dhahab* (vol.3, p.51) it is mentioned:

---

[22] See Shaykh Ahmad ibn Muhammad ad-Dehlawee al-Madanee, *A History of the People of Hadeeth* (Birmingham: Salafi Publications, Ramadān 1425AH/December 2005), p.38

The Shāfi'ī madhhab was spread beyond the river (to Transoxania) by Qaffāl ash-Shāshī. He died in the year 365 AH (1005 AH).

In the *Tāreekh* of Ibn Khallikān, in the second volume, under the biography of an-Nāsir Salāhuddeen Yūsuf ibn Ayyūb, it says:

> When the state of Ayyūbiyyah was set up in the 5th century AH (from circa 1010 CE) in Misr [Egypt], the madhhabs were revived by building schools for its jurists and other means. The Shāfi'ī madhhab was given big favours to make it known and the judges were chosen from it because it was the madhhab of the country. Banu Ayyūb were all Shāfi'iyyah, except 'Īsā ibn al-'Ādil.

Al-Maqrīzī thus states in *al-Khutat* (vol.3, p.344):

> When the naval empire of the Turks succeeded it, its authorities were also Shāfi'ī. It continued acting by judging according to the Shāfi'iyyah law until the Sultanate of Mālik adh-Dhāhir Baybaras brought in judges from all four: they were Hanafī, Shāfi'ī, Mālikī and Hanbalī. This continued until the year 665 AH (1267 CE), until there remained no madhhab in all of the Muslim lands except the four madhhabs and the creed of al-Ash'arī which was all taught to its people in the schools, the Khawānik (Sūfī hospice), prayer rooms and retreats (for the Sūfīs) in all the Islamic states. Enmity was shown to the ones who were partisan to anything else and they were criticised. None would be appointed as judges, nor would anyone's witness be accepted, nor would their proposals be accepted, nor would they be accepted as Imāms or teachers – if they did not blindly follow any one of the four madhhabs! The jurists of these countries gave the ruling,

throughout this period, that it is an obligation to adhere to these madhhabs and that anything else was forbidden. This is the state of affairs up to today.[23]

Sixthly, the Ash'arīs foundation of *Kalām* was attacked and condemned by Shāfi'ī scholars such as adh-Dhahabī, Ibn Katheer, Ibn Hajar and as-Suyūtī all condemning the very *kalām* which Murād (Winter) refers to as enlightened "philosophical thought". How on earth Murād manages to construe that al-Ghazālī, ar-Rāzī and Taftāzānī in some way represent the beliefs of the *Salaf* is beyond us, hence the fragility of contemporary Ash'arite logic.

As for Shaykh ul-Islām Ibn Taymiyyah ﷺ being "imprisoned for heresy" then exactly the same accusation was levelled against Imām Ahmad ibn Hanbal ﷺ who was also accused of heresy by the prevailing heretical Mu'tazilah rulers and their intelligentsia. Imām Mālik ﷺ was also imprisoned, beaten and criticised by the rulers for holding onto his positions. So the mere fact that Shaykh ul-Islām Ibn Taymiyyah was imprisoned and accused of heresy is understandable considering the fact that the Ash'arī creed by the time of Ibn Taymiyyah was becoming more established. It must also be emphasised that even though the Ash'arī inclined intelligentsia had incited the arrest and imprisonment of Shaykh ul-Islām Ibn Taymiyyah the Damascene populace loved him.

As for Hanbalism in some way nurturing "troubled urban masses" and winning their "violent, riotous support" then this can equally be applied to the spread of the Mālikī-Ash'arī[24] school within north-west Africa with the self-proclaimed "Mahdī" Ibn Tumart (d. 1128 CE) and 'AbdulMūmin (d. 1163 CE), who both rebelled and overthrew the al-Murābitūn. Also with the hardcore Hanafism exemplified in the

---

[23] See Shaykh Ahmad ibn Muhammad ad-Dehlawee al-Madanee, op.cit., p.80-86.

[24] I say "*Mālikī-Ash'arī*" because Ibn Tumart was an ardent Ash'arī who endeavoured to institute its creed within Africa and *al-Andalus*. Many *Mālikī fuqahā* were not *Ash'arī*, refer to an interesting piece by Shaykh Mashhūr Hasan on this topic here: http://salafimanhaj.com/pdf/SalafiManhaj_RefuteAsharees.pdf

Muridism of Imām Shāmil of Daghestan (d. 1871 CE) or with the Afghān Tālibān *Tasawwuf* teachers. Not to mention the stringent Shāfi'ism found within Shām and al-Azhar, which extols the virtue of the *Khalaf* over the virtue of the *Salaf*. So Hanbalism in Islamic history has not had a monopoly on "simple literalism" and "violent, riotous support" from "troubled urban masses", as TJ Winter (Abdal-Hakīm Murād) may have us believe. Such ahistoricity therefore is but an example of Orientalism within Western Asharite garb and Winter has unfortunately become renowned for his essentialism[25] when writing about Salafis generally and Saudi Arabia in particular. This method allows polemics to take priority over discussion and argumentation and thus Winter has been rather reluctant to present his contentions when faced with the prospect of directly engaging the *Salafis* in a reasoned and neutral fashion.

It is also obvious that despite their attempts, Ash'arī theologians are evidently unable to draw upon referral to the *Salaf* for their creed, instead referring to those who were only influenced by aspects of the Ash'arī dialectic or obscure scholars about whom little is known. At times it is also evident that the evidence used to advanced their approach is not drawn from an authentic or trusted source This is to emphasise that while Shaykh ul-Islām Ibn Taymiyyah is critiqued, his contemporaries were palpably not to the same meticulous academic level attained by Shaykh ul-Islām Ibn Taymiyyah ﷺ.

The contemporary Ash'arīs also like to refer to Ibn al-Jawzī as if he were in complete harmony and agreement with them. Further investigation however reveals that Ibn ul-Jawzī strongly criticised Abu'l-Hasan al-Ash'arī for delving into *kalām* (speculative-rhetorical discussion). Not only did Ibn ul-Jawzī in his book *Sayd ul-Khātir* criticise al-Ash'arī but also Ibn ul-Jawzī again condemned al-Ash'arī in his book *al-Muntadham* saying:

---

[25] Generalised statements which are asserted that make no reference to possible variations.

He was born in 260 AH. He delved into kalām, and was upon the madhdhab of the Mu'tazilah for a long time. He then decided to oppose them and proclaimed a doctrine which muddled up people's beliefs and caused endless strife. The people never differed that this audible Qur'an is Allah's Speech, and that Gabriel descended with it upon the Prophet ﷺ. The reliable imams declared that the Quran is eternal, while the Mu'tazilah claimed that it is created. Al-Ash'ari then agreed with the Mu'tazilah that the Quran is created and said: 'This is not Allah's Speech. Rather, Allah's Speech is an Attribute subsisting in Allah's Essence. It did not descend on the Prophet, nor is it audible.' Ever since he proclaimed this belief, he lived in fear for his life for opposing the orthodox community (Ahl us-Sunnah), until he sought refuge in the house of Abu al-Hasan al-Tamimi fearing his assassination. Then some of the rulers began to fanatically follow his madhab, and his following increased, until the Shafi'is abandoned the beliefs of al-Shafi'i and instead followed al-Ash'ari's doctrine.[26]

Ibn Katheer also highlights Ibn ul-Jawzī's strong censure of the Ash'arīs in *al-Bidāyah wa'n-Nihāyah* (Beirut: Maktabah al-Ma'ārif), vol.11, p.206. Al-Ash'arī however did finally retract and his later writings on creed: *Maqalāt ul-Islāmiyyeen*, *Risālah ila Ahl ith-Thaghr* and *al-Ibānah 'an il-Usūl id-Diyānah* are testimony to his rejection of speculative-rhetorical discussion and his conformity with the creed of the Salaf. The contemporary Ash'arīs however, have been hesitant to refer to these sources due to the clear agreement with *Salafiyyah* contained within these works authored by Abu'l-Hasan al-Ash'arī. In some instances it has been asserted by some Orientalists and Ash'arīs that these works were

---

[26] Ibn al-Jawzi, *al-Muntadham* (Beirut: Dar al-Fikr, 1995 CE), vol. 8, p.219

merely authored to please the Hanābilah or to deceive them, yet this is unlikely as he was an honest scholar who did not present two-faces in regards to an essential subject such as Islamic theology.

The Ash'arīs therefore have been found wanting in terms of recognising the correct 'aqeedah as inherited from the *Salaf*, so for instance some contemporary Ash'arīs have either admitted to the existence of the Salafī/Atharī 'aqeedah (from whence in the mid-1990s they criticised it!?), or some of them are utilising obscure works to discredit the Salafī 'aqeedah. As for some of the more ominous aspects of the Ash'arī dialectic then this includes the belief that the Qur'ān is created yet that this only be taught within private instruction or within a teaching environment. This in itself is the most clear example of the Ash'arī agreement with Mu'tazilī beliefs and methods in approaching the Islamic texts.

THE 'AQĪDAH OF IMĀM
AN-NAWAWĪ

ABU ZAKARIYYAH YAHYA BIN SHARAF AN-NAWAWI ٱ[27]

---

[27] Since Imām an-Nawawī ٱ is so well known and respected by all Muslims, and not only Salafis, we suffice with a short reminder to the readers of the virtues of this great Imām. Imām Abū Zakariyyah Yahyā Bin Sharaf An-Nawawī was born in the month of Muharram, 631 AH/1234 CE. Indeed, the Imām was granted Allāh's Blessing from a young age; from the time he was young, his father realized his sharpness and keenness, and sent him to memorize the Qur'ān. During his memorizing the Qur'ān, the Qur'ān became beloved to him, and he would hate to part it, to the point that he would not even play with the children of his neighbourhood, and when they did force him to play, and he was 10 years old at the time, he disliked it and began to cry while being forced to play with them! The author of *at-Tabaqāt* comments that when he was merely 19 years old, he travelled to Damascus and learned with the Scholars there; it is mentioned that he used to sit and learn in 12 difference classes a day, such as Jurisprudence, Linguistics, *Usūl*, and so forth. The Imām went on to authoring numerous well-received books, including *al-Arba'īn*, *Riyād-us-Sālihīn*, *al-Mujmū'* and an explanation of *Sahīh Muslim*. Imām adh-Dhahabī mentions him as,

> "The Shaykh, the Imām, the role model, the one who memorizes the Qur'ān and Hadīth, the ascetic, the Jurist, the one who puts out great effort in learning, the one who raises the people on the truth; he is Shaykh al-Islām, the best of his time, the reviver of the religion. He authored books that were sought out from far, and which became popular in the furthest areas of the world."

Imām an-Nawawī died in the year 676 Hijri (1278 CE) ٱ.

[Introduction]

Indeed, all praise is due to Allāh, we praise Him, we seek His aid, and we ask for His forgiveness. We seek refuge in Allāh from the evil of our actions and from the evil consequences of our actions. Whomever Allāh guides, there is none to misguide and whoever Allāh misguides there is none to guide. I bear witness that there is no god worthy of worship except Allāh and I bear witness that Muhammad (ﷺ) is the servant and messenger of Allāh.

[Imam an-Nawawi's Reliance on al-Qadi 'Iyyad]

In regards to al-Qādī 'Iyyād's *ta'weel* of Allāh's *'Uluww* when Imām an-Nawawī ﷺ transmitted from him, I wanted to eulogize and compile what has been mentioned in regards to the 'aqeedah of Imām an-Nawawī ﷺ. There are some people who go to excess with regards to an-Nawawī ﷺ to the extent that some extremists have obligated that his *Sharh* of Saheeh Muslim should be burnt. Nawawī ﷺ, in more than one instance, as I indicated in the last lesson, views that the 'aqeedah of the Salaf revolves between *tafweedh* (of the meaning) or *ta'weel*. In this he traversed the way of those *'Ulama* who preceded him and from whom he

transmitted, like those whose books he transmitted from, and as you have seen with Imām an-Nawawī's statements regarding *istiwā'* he merely depended upon what was stated by al-Qāḍī 'Iyyāḍ in *Ikmal ul-Mu'lim*. And I have mentioned to you that whenever al-Qāḍī 'Iyyāḍ himself states: **"The Imām said..."** he intends by that al-Māzarī. Al-Māzarī was a pure 'Ash'arī as opposed to al-Qāḍī 'Iyyāḍ who was in-between, yet the context and position prevented him from taking the Attributes upon their apparent meaning. I have stated in a number of instances that an-Nawawī ﷺ transmits from al-Qāḍī 'Iyyāḍ's *Ikmal ul-Mu'lim* and attributes that to him and we have already seen that whenever al-Qāḍī 'Iyyāḍ has been preceded in anything he will state: *"the Imām said..."* referring to al-Māzarī.

[The Omissions by Past Copyists of Imam an-Nawawi's Creed]

I repeat again and say that an-Nawawī ﷺ at times in his books fell into *ta'weel* of some of Allāh's Attributes and this can particularly be seen in his *Sharh* of Saheeh Muslim. This did not please some copyists of his *Sharh* of Saheeh Muslim who were close to his time. As a result, some copyists who had a Salafī 'aqeedah copied an-Nawawī's *Sharh* and left

out from their copies the places where an-Nawawī makes *ta'weel* of Allāh's Attributes.

[The Critique of Ibn as-Subki]

Ibn as-Subkī became angered at this and had some stern words for those copyists, he stated in *Tabaqāt ush-Shāfi'iyyah al-Kubrā*, vol.2, p.19:

> Some of the Mujassimah of our time[28] have gone to the extent that they have copied out the Sharh of Saheeh Muslim by Shaykh Muhiyuddeen an-Nawawī and omitted an-Nawawī's words wherein he mentions the ahādeeth of Allāh's Attributes. For indeed an-Nawawī was 'Ash'arī in 'aqeedah yet the copyist could not handle writing what the classifier of the work (i.e. an-Nawawī) had mentioned.

Ibn-us-Subkī was of the main enemies of Shaykh ul-Islām (Ibn Taymiyyah) and he was the one who incited his imprisonment, he was a judge, may Allāh forgive him. Then Ibn us-Subkī appended to this, in

---

[28] [TN]: Ibn as-Subkī, was motivated by polemics in much of his writings about those who emphasised the 'aqeedah of the Salaf hence the use of slurs such as "*Mujassim*" towards those who have not actually committed *tajseem*, and with neither evidence of the existence of such *tajseem* nor a detailed assessment of the beliefs of the alleged proponents of *tajseem*.

regards to the copyist who left out sections of an-Nawawī's words in regards to *ahādeeth* in his *Sharh* of Saheeh Muslim:

> With me this is of the major sins, for indeed this is tahreef of the Sharee'ah and opening up a door which is not safe to people's books and the classifications that they possess. May Allāh disgrace the one who does this, he was in no need of this Sharh and the Sharh was in no need of him.

Then I also found these same words of his within his book *Qā'idah fi'l-Jarh wa't-Ta'deel*, p.48 except that the editor and commentator of the book, despite being a Hanafī in *madhhab* and 'Ash'arī in creed, states in regards to what Ibn us-Subkī stated above:

> Yes, this would be correct if he (the copyist) did not bring attention to this in the book or in the introduction of the book. As for when he does bring attention to his method in an abridged manner within the book in a way which can be understood then there is nothing on him (i.e. the copyist). The author (i.e. Ibn us-Subkī) went to excess in this matter, may Allāh forgive me and him.

Yes, as-Subkī went overboard in his critique of the copyist and the copyist, may Allāh increase him in goodness, did not want the people of *bāṭil* to assume power via referral to the words of an-Nawawī ﷺ.

[Imam an-Nawawi's Instruction to Ibn 'Attar]

An-Nawawī ﷺ has been described by some Shāfiʿī *ʿUlama*, such as as-Suyūṭī in his treatise *al-Minhāj us-Sawī fī Tarjamat in-Nawawī*. An-Nawawī instructed his main student "Ibn 'Attār" 'Aluddeen Ibrāheem bin 'Ali to erase a large body of his books. He stated:

> I did as he instructed and within myself I was regretful about what I did, to the extent that he instructed me to blot out Minhāj ut-Tālibeen so I took him up on this and stated to him that 'the book has become widespread among students so what is the benefit of erasing it?' Then Imām an-Nawawī remained silent.

Ibn 'Attār was named the "*Mukhtasar of an-Nawawī*" and he is the brother of Imām adh-Dhahabī by suckling. He was also a contemporary of Shaykh ul-Islām (Ibn Taymiyyah) as opposed to an-Nawawī. An-Nawawī was a contemporary of Majd-ud-deen, the grandfather of

Shaykh ul-Islām, as for Ahmad bin 'Abdul-Haleem Abu'l'Abbās Ibn Taymiyyah then he was not a contemporary of an-Nawawī. On this note, there is a book available in the markets entitled *Mawāqif Butooliyyah min Sun'at il-Islām* wherein the author claims that an-Nawawī met Ibn Taymiyyah and praised him etc. Yet upon inspection this holds no weight, this is imagination.

[Analysing the Claim that Imam an-Nawawi was 'Ash'ari in Creed]

Let's return, what did Ibn us-Subkī say about an-Nawawī? That he was 'Ash'arī. This is common to find from as-Subkī for he transmitted in the first volume of *Tabaqāt ush-Shāfi'iyyah*, p.132 statements of an-Nawawī in regards to *īmān* and then states that an-Nawawī was 'Ash'arī in *'aqeedah*. As for adh-Dhahabī, who was of the more trustworthy Shaykhs of the historians, then he gave a biography of an-Nawawī in *as-Siyar* which has been printed yet the biography, along with the biography of Ibn Taymiyyah, have been lost. *As-Siyar* is incomplete from the end of it and there are no two manuscript copies of it. As-Sakhāwī within his biography of an-Nawawī transmits adh-Dhahabī's statements from *as-Siyar* yet when we refer back to *as-Siyar* we do not find the biography of

an-Nawawī. The copyist of *al-Awāsim* by Ibn Wazeer transmits within the marginal notes from *Siyar A'lam un-Nubalā* that: **"I found the biography of Shaykh ul-Islām Ibn Taymiyyah in *as-Siyar* and this is it here..."** and then he relays it letter for letter and word for word. So may Allāh reward the copyist of *al-Awāsim* by Ibn Wazeer with good for he relayed the biography of Ibn Taymiyyah from *as-Siyar* and this book has been printed and published. As for the biography of an-Nawawī from *as-Siyar* then we only have parts of it that have been relayed by as-Sakhāwī. However, when Dr Bashhār 'Awād printed *Tāreekh ul-Islām*, and he managed to obtain a manuscript copy of it, a biography of Imām an-Nawawī is found within *Tāreekh ul-Islām*, and there are also words from adh-Dhahabī in regards to the 'aqeedah of an-Nawawī.

[The Statement of adh-Dhahabi regarding an-Nawawi's Creed]

In *Tāreekh ul-Islām* (Dār ul-Gharb print), vol.15, p.332 adh-Dhahabī states about an-Nawawī:

His madhhab in regards to the Attributes was to remain silent and accept them as they have arrived, and perhaps he may

have made some slight ta'weel within his Sharh of Saheeh Muslim.

These words can be applied to the reality, correct? This totally agrees with the reality of the matter. There are also some words which are found within the manuscript of *Tāreekh ul-Islām*:

So an-Nawawī was a man who was 'Ash'arī in 'aqeedah and well known for this, he made tabdī' of those who opposed him and was stern against them.

The editor and checker of *Tāreekh ul-Islām*, our friend Bashhār states with regards to the expression: **"an-Nawawī was a man who was 'Ash'arī in 'aqeedah"** that: **"This sentence was written by the classifier/copyist in the marginal notes"**, and I say: this expression is not from adh-Dhahabī because there is a clash, and rather a contradiction, between the two sentences! Also, an-Nawawī was calm in his nature, he safeguarded what his tongue said and he was not harsh in his words. Therefore, to say:

So an-Nawawī was a man who was 'Ash'arī in 'aqeedah and well known for this, he made tabdī' of those who opposed him and was stern against them.

Is not correct, for it opposes what is in his books. My Lord facilitated it for me to obtain a piece of the end of the manuscript of *Tāreekh ul-Islām* from *Khuda Baksh Library* in India[29] which contains a biography of an-Nawawī and the sentence (which claims that an-Nawawī was 'Ash'arī) is not found therein and all praise is due to Allāh. Then I referred to the biography of an-Nawawee by as-Sakhāwee and he relayed his *madhhab* and abridged what adh-Dhahabī stated when he said: "and perhaps he may have made some slight ta'weel within his Sharh of *Saheeh Muslim.*"

[Ibn 'Attar Abandons the 'Ash'ari Creed]

Therefore, an-Nawawī ﷺ was influenced (by the 'Ash'arīs) in some matters and in some instances he fell into *ta'weel*. Dar ul-Kutub ul-Misriyyah in Cairo recently printed a book entitled *Juzun fihi Dhikr I'tiqād us-Salaf fi-Hurūf wa'l-Aswāt* which is of the works of Imām an-

---

[29] [TN]: Located in Patna (in Bihar state in Eastern India) it is one of the national libraries in India and it holds a very rare collection of Arabic and Persian manuscripts and folios. It was opened in October 1891 CE by Bihar Khan Khuda Baksh with 4000 manuscripts, 1400 of these were inherited from his father Muhammad Baksh. Currently the repository holds some 21,000 manuscripts. In 1969 the Indian government declared the library an 'Institution of National Importance', the library is now fully funded by the Indian Ministry of Culture. Refer to: http://kblibrary.bih.nic.in/default.htm

Nawawī. In the end of the section it is mentioned: "We finished copying the book on Thursday 3 Rabī' ul-Awwal 677 AH (CE)." Ibn 'Attār mentions, and he stayed with an-Nawawī for six years and I forgot to mention to you that when Ibn 'Attār met *Shaykh ul-Islām* Ibn Taymiyyah he retracted from what he had picked up from an-Nawawī and he authored a good work entitled *al-I'tiqād fī Nafiyi Shakk wa Irtiyāb* wherein he firmly establishes and acknowledges the *'aqeedah* of Ahl us-Sunnah, the *'aqeedah* of the Salaf and refutes the 'Ashā'irah. This has been published the *tahqeeq* of our brother, the respected Shaykh 'Ali al-Halabī.[30]

[The Creed of an-Nawawi Regarding Allah's Speech]

Let's return, this portion copied from an-Nawawī was completed on Thursday 2 Rabī al-Awwal 677 AH and Ibn 'Attār has a huge biography of Imām an-Nawawī entitled *Tuhfat it-Tālibeen fī Tarjamatil-Imām il-Muhyiddeen*. It was facilitated for me to obtain a copy of this from the *Awqaf* of Halab (Aleppo) which was written in the handwriting of his brother. All praise is due to Allāh this has been printed and published

---

[30] [TN]: The book is also referred to by the title *I'tiqād ul-Khālis*.

and I completed this about ten years ago.[31] Ibn 'Attār states in *Tuhfat ut-Tālibeen*: "An-Nawawī died in the last third of the night of Wednesday 24 Rajab 676 AH in Nawaw." So an-Nawawī completed the aforementioned book on the third of Muharram 676 AH and an-Nawawī died in 676 AH so this work is of the last works that Imām an-Nawawī authored. So the gap between his death and this work is only that of seven months, as Muharram is the first month and Rajab is the seventh month. We do not know of a work that he authored after this. Listen to what is mentioned in this book, I will read a section of it unto you, an-Nawawī states after noting what the 'Ash'arīs say about Allāh's Speech:

It is amazing that the books of the 'Ashā'irah state the Speech of Allāh was revealed upon the Prophet, is written in the masāhif, recited upon the tongues in a real sense and then they still say: 'that which has been revealed is an expression; that which is written is not the writing (of the Qur'ān); that which is recited is not the recitation (of the Qur'ān)' – thus explaining the matter with apparent contradictions and weak and discreet commentaries. It is sufficient in refuting these beliefs that they are unable to clearly state such beliefs, rather they are in a type of dispute (over the beliefs themselves).

---

[31] Riyadh: Dār us-Sumay'ī, 1414 AH/1993 CE

THE 'AQĪDAH OF IMĀM AN-NAWAWĪ

The 'Ash'arīs say that Allāh's Speech is *Nafsī* (Internal) and that the Qur'ān which is within our hands is created, however they do not come out openly and clearly with this (belief). Yet some of their contemporary scholars have openly stated this, a proof for this is in the fact that one of their later scholars al-Bayjūrī stated in *Sharh ul-Jawharah*[32], p.94, mentions: *"is the Qur'ān better or Sayyidina Muhammad ﷺ?"* he then indicates the difference of opinion in this matter according to them (i.e. the 'Ash'arīs) and then says: *"The truth is that Muhammad ﷺ is better because he is the best of all creation."* What does this mean? This means that the Qur'ān [according to them] is created. Shaykh ul-Islām Ibn Taymiyyah in *Majmū' al-Fatāwā*, vol.12, pp.424-425 has some amazing words wherein he refutes the 'Ash'arīs and explains that the Qur'ān according to them (i.e. the 'Ash'arīs) is but ink and paper and their own predecessors stated this. Ibn Taymiyyah stated:

Then some followers of the 'Ash'arīs came along and said that the Qur'ān is only established in Allāh's Essence (i.e. 'internal') and that the Letters are not from Allāh's Speech, rather Allāh created them in the air or they were compiled by Jibreel or Muhammad. They thus added to this that the Mus-

---

[32] [TN]: This is a well-known *'Ash'arī* didactical text on *'tawhīd'* which contains neither an *ayah* nor a *hadīth*! See: http://marifah.net/articles/JawharatalTawhid.pdf

haf contains nothing but ink and paper and that based on what their predecessors had stated is just an evidence of Allāh's Speech which has to be respected. Yet when they began to view that the Mus-haf is an 'evidence' (of Allāh's Speech) it therefore does not obligate any respect as all things in existence are a proof of Allāh yet do not necessitate respect. As a result, these 'Ash'arīs began to belittle the Mus-haf to the extent that they would kick it with their feet and some of them would even write Allāh's Names with filth all in order to belittle the honour of Allāh's Names and His Verses that are written in the Masāhif and on paper. The Muslims have agreed that whoever belittles the Mus-haf by throwing it into filth or kicks it — is a disbeliever whom it is permissible to execute. An innovation begins slowly by a hand-span and then it increases till it grows.

So what can be observed is that an-Nawawī was surprised at what the 'Ash'arīs stated about Allāh's Attribute of Speech as he stated on page 53 (of al-I'tiqād) after discussing the Attribute of Speech. He then states on page 62 after transmitting from Imam Ahmad who said "*may Allāh curse the Mushabbihah and the Mu'attilah*":

So it was said to him: "who are the Mushabbihah?" He said: "Those who say, 'Hand like my hand, seeing like my seeing.'"

Then he transmitted from Ahmad that he said: "Whoever resembles Allāh with His creation is a disbeliever in Allāh", then he said:

Our madhhab is between the two madhhabs, guidance between the two forms of misguidance, affirmation of the Names and Attributes along with negating tashbeeh and bodily forms. We do not go to excess with the Attributes and make them like a body in doing so resembling Allāh to His creation, exalted is Allāh over this. Likewise, we are not deficient in regards to the Attributes by negating what Allāh affirmed for Himself, rather we say what we have heard and we testify to what we know.

[The Creed of an-Nawawi Regarding Allah's Attributes]

He then said on page 63 after relaying Allāh's statement:

﴿ لَيْسَ كَمِثْلِهِۦ شَىْءٌ وَهُوَ ٱلسَّمِيعُ ٱلْبَصِيرُ ﴾ ⟨١⟩

"*There is nothing like unto Him and He is the Hearing, the Seeing*"

(42:11):

We describe and do not resemble, we affirm and not ascribe bodily forms, we know and we do not ask "how?" Our

madhhab is between the two madhhabs, guidance between the two forms of misguidance, a Sunnah between two innovations, Allāh is Unique in His Attributes. We believe in them, we have certainty in their realities and we are ignorant as to the knowledge of "how" the Attributes are.

How beautiful are these words! This is the 'aqeedah of the Salaf! Then he stated on page 67:

From our deen we hold firm to the Book of Allāh, Mighty and Majestic, and to the Sunnah of our Prophet ﷺ and what has been reported from the Companions and the Tābi'een, and the famous Imāms of Hadeeth; and we believe in all of the ahadeeth of Allāh's Attributes. We neither add anything at all to that nor decrease anything from that. Like the hadeeth regarding the Dajjāl wherein it is stated: "And indeed your Lord is not one-eyed"; and like the hadeeth of Nuzool to the heavens of the Dunya; and like the hadeeth of Istiwā above the 'Arsh; and that the hearts are between His Two Fingers; and that He will place the Heavens on His Finger and the two earths on His Finger; and we affirm the ahādeeth of the Mi'rāj.

Then he stated:

We believe that Allāh is above His 'Arsh, as He informed in His Mighty Book and we do not say that "He is everywhere", rather He is above the Heavens and His Knowledge is everywhere. No place conceals Him as He said: "Do you feel safe from He who is above the Heavens..." and as He said: "To Him ascends good speech..."; and as is mentioned in the hadeeth of Isrā' that he ﷺ went up to the seven heavens to his Lord and then came down; and as is found in the hadeeth of the black lady who wanted to be freed and the Prophet ﷺ said to her: "Where is your Lord?" And she replied: "Above the heavens" and then the Prophet ﷺ said: "Free her for indeed she is a believer." The examples of this are many within the Book and the Sunnah. We believe in that and we do not reject any of that. The thiqāt have narrated from Mālik bin Anas that someone asked him about the Saying of Allāh:

﴿ ٱلرَّحْمَـٰنُ عَلَى ٱلْعَرْشِ ٱسْتَوَىٰ ۩ ﴾

'Ar-Rahmān established Himself over the 'Arsh' (20:5) and then replied: 'al-Istiwā' is not majhool (unknown) and the 'how' is not ma'qool (comprehended), believing in it is obligatory and asking about it is an innovation.'

[The Transmission of Abul-Hasan al-'Ash'ari's Creed by Imam an-Nawawi]

This is the first evidence, the second evidence is what I found within *Majmoo' al-Fatāwā*, vol.3, p.224 of Shaykh ul-Islām Ibn Taymiyyah 拢, for he debated, defended, authored and held gatherings on *tawheed* and especially on Allāh's Names and Attributes. Speaking about himself he says:

> When we gathered in Damascus and the books of Abu'l-Hasan al-'Ash'arī were presented such as al-Maqalāt and al-Ibānah, and likewise the books of his companions such as al-Qādī Abū Bakr (al-Bāqilānī), Ibn Fawrak, al-Bayhaqī and others, and his book al-Ibānah was presented as was what was mentioned by Ibn Asākir in his book Tabyeen Kadhib al-Muftarī fimā Nusiba ila'l-'Ash'arī, and this was transmitted from him (Abu'l-Hasan al-'Ash'arī) in Aboo Zakariyya an-Nawawī's own handwriting. Abu'l-Hasan al-'Ash'arī said within it (i.e. al-Ibānah): 'So if it is said: "If you have rejected the sayings of the Mu'tazilah, Qadariyyah, Jahmiyyah, Harooriyyah, Rāfidah, Murji'ah then let us know about the

view which you say." Say to him: "Our saying is: holding firm to the Book of Allāh and the Sunnah of His Messenger ﷺ and what was related from the Companions, Successors and the Imāms of hadeeth. We adhere firmly to this and what was stated by Ahmad bin Hanbal, may Allāh enlighten his face and may Allāh raise his station and increase his reward, and we stay away from opposing his view because he is a virtuous Imām with whom Allāh clarified the truth when misguidance emerged, made the minhāj clear and suppressed the innovators, deviants and doubters." Then he (Abu'l-Hasan al-'Ash'arī) stated: 'Chapter: In Regards to Istiwā': So if someone says: "What do you say about istiwā'?" Say to him: 'Allāh is Established (Mustawi') over His Throne as Allāh has said:

$$ \text{﴿ ٱلرَّحْمَٰنُ عَلَى ٱلْعَرْشِ ٱسْتَوَىٰ ۝ ﴾} $$

"The Most Merciful [who is] above the Throne established."
(20:5) And Allāh says,

$$ \text{﴿ إِلَيْهِ يَصْعَدُ ٱلْكَلِمُ ٱلطَّيِّبُ ﴾} $$

"To Him ascends good speech..." (35:10)[33] And Allāh says,

---

[33] [TN]: Ibn Katheer mentioned in his *Tafsīr* it means: words of remembrance, recitation of Qur'ān, and supplications. This was the view of more than one of the Salaf. Ibn Jareer recorded that Al-Mukhāriq bin Sulaym said that "'Abdullāh bin Mas'ood ؓ said to them, "If we tell you a hadeeth, we will bring you proof of it from the Book of Allāh.

﴿ بَل رَّفَعَهُ ٱللَّهُ إِلَيْهِ ﴾

"Rather, Allāh raised him to Himself." (4:158)[34]

This is all transmitted by an-Nawawī in his own handwriting from Abu'l-Hasan al-'Ash'arī, this is a second proof.

[The Creed of Imam an-Nawawi Regarding *Istiwa* and his Support of al-Khattabi]

The third evidence is the admiration and adoration that Imām an-Nawawī had of al-Khattābī. There is a book entitled *Tabaqāt ul-Fuqahā ush-Shāfi'iyyah* authored by Ibn us-Salāh which was commented upon, arranged and distributed by an-Nawawī. An-Nawawī stated in his commentary on it, vol.1, p.470 under the biography of al-Khattābī:

When the Muslim servants says, 'Glory and praise be to Allāh, there is no god worthy of worship except Allāh, Allāh is Most Great and blessed be Allāh,' an angel takes these words and puts them under his wing, then he ascends with them to the heaven. He does not take them past any group of angels but they seek forgiveness for the one who said them, until he brings them before Allāh, may He be glorified." Refer to the online version of *Tafsīr*:
http://www.qtafsir.com/index.php?option=com_content&task=view&id=1912&Itemid=91
[34] [TN]: related to this are the many *ahādīth* which states that Īsā ﷺ will "descend" and be "sent down" from whence Allāh raised him to. So this also indicates the *fawqiyyah* (above-ness) of Allāh.

Al-Khattābī mentioned clearly that Allāh is above the heavens and some of them say that istiwā here is 'isteela' and they argue the case with an unknown line of poetry which is not correct to use.[35]

---

35 [TN]: The false interpretation of "isteela" (i.e. "He conquered the Throne") was initially asserted by Qādī 'Abdul-Jabbār the founder of *Mu'tazilī* thought and then taken on board by the 'Ash'arīs. Yet this interpretation is invalid from a number of aspects:
• The Arabic language does not allow that the meaning of "Istawā" is "isteelā", and this meaning is not quoted from any of the trusted Imāms of Arabic linguistics, rather it has been authentically transmitted from them that they totally rejected this meaning. Take for example, Abū 'Abdullāh Muhammad bin Ziyād Ibn al-A'rābī (d. 231 AH/845 CE), who was the son of a Sindi slave and the foster-child of the famous Kufan philologist, al-Mufaddal bin Muhammad ad-Dabbī. His prodigious memory was a storehouse of Arabic philology, folklore and poetry. He was an Imām in Arabic linguistics and philology who questioned al-Asma'ī and Abū 'Ubaydah Ma'mar bin al-Muthanna. Some fragments of his works are present in the collection of manuscripts collected by the Royal Netherlands Academy of Arts and Sciences in Amsterdam, refer to its inventory here: http://www.islamicmanuscripts.info/inventories/amsterdam/inventory-academy-collection.pdf. He is not to be confused with Abū Sa'eed Ahmad ibn Muhammad ibn Ziyād ibn Bishr ibn al-A'rābī (d. 341 AH/952 CE) from Basra and then Makkah, who was the student of Abū Dāwūd as-Sijistānī and author of Kitāb ul-Mu'jam, Ibn Abī Zayd narrated from.
Ibn al-A'rābī said (as reported in Khateeb al-Baghdādī, *Tāreekh Baghdād*, vol.5, p.283 and al-Lālikā'ī, *Sharh Usul I'tiqād*, vol.3, p.399 with a *sahīh sanad*): "Ibn Abī Dāwood wished that I seek out some of the phrases of the Arabs and their meanings. (So he said): **"the Most Merciful Istawā upon the Throne"** (20:5) *"Istawā"* meaning *"Istawlā"*? I said to him, "By Allāh, this does not mean this and I have never seen this." Al-Khaleel ibn Ahmad was asked: "Have you seen in the language *'Istawā'* taken to mean *'Istawlā'*?" To which he replied, "This is neither known to the Arab nor possible in the language." This is why Ibn al-Jawzī says in *Zād al-Maseer*, vol.3, p.213: "This meaning is rejected according to the linguists." Ibn Abdul Barr said in *at-Tamhīd*, vol.7, p.131: "Their saying in explanation of *Istiwā* that it means *Isteelā* is not correct in the language." This false meaning was mentioned by the later grammarians who inherited this understanding from the *Mu'tazilah* and the *Jahmiyyah*. They did not rely upon narrations for this view; rather they relied on the alleged saying of the poet, *"istawā Bishrun 'ala'l-'Irāq"*. This was

He also mentioned that al-Khattābī had a treatise entitled *ar-Risālah an-Nāsihah fimā yu'taqidu fi's-Sifāt*. Therefore, an-Nawawī transmitted the words of al-Khattābī regarding Allāh being over the heavens and that Allāh is Established over His Throne and these references were in relation to praising al-Khattābī. So if an-Nawawī did not accept these words of al-Khattābī then he would have either distorted them or he

---

utilised by GF Haddād in *Islamic Belief and Doctrine According to Ahl al-Sunna, Vol.1: A Repudiation of "Salafi" Innovations* (Mountain View, CA: ASFA, 1996), p.106 – the book has Hisham Kabbānī's name on the cover yet was more than likely penned by GF Haddād whose name appears inside as 'editor'! The following have to be taken into account: ● This line of poetry is not classed as being an authentic Arabic poem because it has not been transmitted via a credible route. It is neither referred to nor found in any collections of Arabic poetry, and cannot be traced. ● There is no known origin in history for this line, and neither is there any indication in this line that would show that the poet meant *istawā* with the meaning of *istawlā* such that it could be depended upon. ● (It is possible that) this poem is distorted and its correct phraseology is, *"Bishrun qad istawlā 'ala'l-'Irāq"*. ● Even if this poem is authentic and it is not distorted then it still is not a proof for them, rather it is against them because Bishr was the brother of the Khaleefah al-Umawī (the Umayyad Caliph) 'AbdulMalik bin Marwān, and he (Bishr) was the Ameer of 'Irāq and he made *Istawā* upon it as was the habit of the leaders that they sit above the throne of the kingdom, and this conforms to the meaning of this word as mentioned in His, the Exalted, saying, **"...that you may mount upon their backs (*li tastawū alā dhuhoorihī*)"** (43):14)
Ibn al-A'rābī said: "He is on His Throne as He has told us." He said, "O Abu 'Abdullāh, does it not mean *istawlā* (possess, take control)?" Ibn al-A'rābī said: "How can you know that? The Arabs do not say *istawlā* unless there are two people competing for a throne, then whichever of them prevails, they describe as *istawlā*." Refer to *Lisān al-'Arab*, vol.2, p.249.
Refer to Online paper by Aboo Rumaysah entitled *A Comparison of the Ta'weels of the Mu'tazilah to the Ta'weels of the Later Ash'arīs*.

would have commented upon them and refuted them. This is the third proof (of an-Nawawī's 'aqeedah).

The fourth evidence: an-Nawawī stated in his book *Rawdat ut-Tālibeen*, which is a *fiqh* book and is of the most famous Shāfi'ī books of *fiqh*. An-Nawawī said in vol.10, p.85 (al-Maktabah al-Islami Print):

> If it is said (by a disbeliever): 'There is no god worthy of worship except Allāh, the King who is above the heavens' or if he says: 'There is no god worthy of worship except the King of the heavens' then such a person who says this is a believer. Allāh says,

> ﴾ أَءَأَمِنتُم مَّن فِى ٱلسَّمَآءِ ﴿

> "Do you feel secure that He who [holds authority] in the heaven..." (67:16) And if he (i.e. the disbeliever) says: 'There is none worthy of worship except the Dweller of the heavens' then he will not be a believer because dwelling is impossible for Allāh, the Mighty and Majestic.

This is correct and this is what Shaykh ul-Islām Ibn Taymiyyah states in *Bayān Talbees ul-Jahmiyyah*, vol.1, p.146. This is also what is stated by Abū Nasr 'Ubaydillāh as-Sijzī al-Wā'ilī (d. 444 AH) in his treatise to the

people of Zabeed entitled *Radd 'alā Man Ankara Harf wa's-Sawt* wherein he stated:

> It is not from our saying that when we say Allāh is above His Throne that we intend a restricted limit for Him, because limits are only for invented things. From the 'Arsh to what is beneath it is that which is restricted and Allāh, Mighty and Majestic, is above that, which is not a 'place' or limit. This is with our agreement that Allāh was there without a place, then he created 'places' and He was as He was before 'places' were created. The only ones who say there is a limited restriction are those who claim that Allāh is in a place, yet it is known that 'places' are restricted, so their claim would mean that Allāh is restricted and according to us Allāh is distinct from 'places' and their limits. Rather, Allāh is above all things that have been brought into existence and according to our saying His Essence has no restriction.

This all agrees with what an-Nawawī stated when he said:

> If he (i.e. the disbeliever) says: 'There is none worthy of worship except the Dweller of the heavens' then he will not be a believer but if he says: 'There is no god worthy of worship except Allāh, the King who is above the heavens' or if he says:

'There is no god worthy of worship except the King of the heavens' then such a person who says this is a believer.

Which indicates that an-Nawawī affirms Allāh's *'Uluww*.

[The Final Word]

These are the four proofs (about Nawawī's true 'aqeedah) so memorise them and know that the final statements of an-Nawawī before his death by a few months demonstrate a return to the Salaf's creed and that he stated what the *Salaf* viewed. So we can affirm that Imām an-Nawawī returned to the 'aqeedah of the *Salaf us-Sālih* and also from what we have read is not from an-Nawawī's own view but rather from what he transmitted from al-Qādī 'Iyyād, yet an-Nawawī himself affirmed what was contrary.

And all praise is due to Allāh

Appendix I: Conclusions on the 'Aqīdah of Imām an-Nawawī

We have seen therefore that it would be wholly inaccurate to consider Imām an-Nawawī ﷺ "an Ash'arī", even though within some of his *Sharh* of Saheeh Muslim he makes *ta'weel* of the *Sifāt*. Yet within Imām an-Nawawī's *Sharh*, he also makes *tafweedh* (of the meaning of the *Sifāt*) and at other times remains silent and adopts the position of the *Salaf*. So for example, in his *Sharh* of Saheeh Muslim he appears to reject al-Qāḍī 'Iyyāḍ's[36] *ta'weel* of Allāh's Hand and states that it should be left alone and not interpreted.[37]

Moreover, some contemporary Ash'arīs have taken issue with later scholars disagreeing with the errors of scholars like Imām an-Nawawī ﷺ, yet these very same Ash'arīs also disagree with, and contradict, Imām an-Nawawī in many issues. Such as:

❖ **Building Masājid on Graves:-** Imām an-Nawawī was asked about a Muslim cemetery upon which is a Masjid with a *Mihrāb* and if this was permissible or not or should they be destroyed?

---

[36] He is Imām, al-'Allāmah, al-Hāfidh, Shaykh ul-Islām, al-Qāḍī Abu'l-Fadl 'Iyyād bin Mūsā bin 'Iyyād bin 'Amru bin Mūsā bin 'Iyyād al-Yahsubī al-Andalūsī as-Sabtī al-Mālikī (476-544 AH), see adh-Dhahabī, *Siyar A'lām un-Nubalā*.

[37] Imām an-Nawawī, *Sharh Sahīh Muslim*, vol.17, p.132

Imām an-Nawawī replied: "That is impermissible, it has to be destroyed."[38]

❖ Prostration to Shaykhs:- Imām an-Nawawī was asked about the prostrating of some people to Shaykhs and the like, what is the ruling on this? Imām an-Nawawī replied: "This is harām, it is severely prohibited."[39] Imām an-Nawawī also stated: "This is definitely *harām* in all cases...some aspects of this necessitate *kufr*, may Allāh protect us."[40]

❖ Innovations Committed at the Prophet's ﷺ Grave:- Imām an-Nawawī stated about the objectionable practices that some people do at the grave of our beloved Prophet ﷺ: "It is not permissible to circumbulate his grave (ﷺ) and it is disliked to touch his grave with the hand or to kiss the grave of the Prophet (ﷺ). Rather, it is good etiquette to refrain from this, as one would refrain from this if one was present during his time. This accurate view has been stated by the Ulamā and they acted upon this. One should not be deceived by the contrary actions performed by common-folk, as guidance and action is only within the sahīh hadīth and the

---

[38] Fatāwā al-Imām an-Nawawī, pp.67-68
[39] Fatāwā al-Imām an-Nawawī, p.76
[40] Imām an-Nawawī, *Rawdat ut-Tālibeen*, vol.1, p.326

statements of the 'Ulamā and one should not turn to the newly-invented matters of common folk or others and their ignorant practices."[41] Imām an-Nawawī also stated: "It is dangerous to touch the grave for Barakah (blessing), this is from ignorance and heedlessness. For Barakah is only in that which agrees with the Shar', how can there be any virtue in opposing what is correct?!"[42]

❖ **Warning Against Deviant Sects:-** Imām an-Nawawī also warned against many deviant views of different sects of innovation such as the *Qadariyyah*,[43] *Mu'tazilah*,[44] *Khawārij* and *Rawāfid*.

What is important to note is that the criteria is the Qur'ān, Sunnah and *Salaf* regardless of who relays it as the later scholars are not at all considered to be infallible. Secondly, if the modern Ash'arīs are free to disagree with Imām an-Nawawī ﷺ, then so are others.

Our Shaykh, Mashhūr Hasan Āl Salmān, in his book *ar-Rudūd wa't-Ta'aqqubāt* (ath-Thuqba, KSA: Dār ul-Hijrah, 1993), p.20 highlights that Imam an-Nawawī did not write an independent work on creed and there are some doubts as to whether the book entitled *al-Maqāsid*, which

---

[41] Imām an-Nawawī, *al-Majmū'*, vol.8, p.275
[42] Ibid., vol.8, p.375
[43] Imām an-Nawawī, *Sharh Sahīh Muslim*, vol.1, pp.154, 156
[44] Ibid., vol.1, pp.109-110, 211

is ascribed to Imām an-Nawawī, was authored by him. The book al-*Maqāsid* has regrettably been translated into English by Nūh Keller, yet as we will see there are some problems with ascribing this work to Imām an-Nawawī. Khayruddeen az-Zirikilī mentions among an-Nawawī's works *al-Maqāsid* and that it is a work on *tawheed*.[45] Ibn ʾAttār does not mention *al-Maqāsid* in his abridged discussion on Imām an-Nawawī's writings.[46] Neither Imāms adh-Dhahabī in *Tadhkirat ul-Huffādh* nor Ibn Katheer in *al-Bidāyah waʾn-Nihāyah* (Beirut: Dār ul-Kutub al-ʾIlmiyyah, 1985 CE), vol.13, in their mention of the works that Imām an-Nawawī began and did not complete, mention *al-Maqāsid* which if indeed was a famous work of Nawawī's on creed they would have highlighted it in numerous writings. Also Imām as-Suyūtī in *al-Minhāj*, pp.53-65 did not mention *al-Maqāsid* in his discussion of the works of Imām an-Nawawī. Ahmad al-Haddād in his writings on the works of Imām an-Nawawī and those which are still in manuscript form did not mention *al-Maqāsid*. Similarly, Hītū, a specialist in Shāfiʿī *fiqh*, did not mention *al-Maqāsid* in his list of 38 works of Imām an-Nawawī.[47] Hence, it can be safely said that *al-Maqāsid*, which has been translated into English by Keller, was ascribed to Imām an-Nawawī but was most likely written by a hardcore

---

[45] Khayruddeen az-Zirikilī, *al-Aʿlām* (Beirut: Dār ul-ʾIlm ul-Malayeen, n.d.), vol.8, p.149
[46] Ibn al-Attār, pp.75-100
[47] Muhammad Hasan Hītū (ed.), Yahyā an-Nawawī, *al-Usūl waʾd-Dawābit* (Beirut: Dār ul-Bashāʾir al-Islāmiyyah, 1988), pp.14-16

Ash'arī who then put Imām an-Nawawī's name on it in order to give it further credibility.[48] Why it can be deduced that Imām an-Nawawī was not an Ash'arī is based on the fact that he was not consistent in his methodology when it came to discussing Allāh's Attributes.

Shaykh Mashhūr notes[49] that Imām an-Nawawī fluctuated between affirmation of Allāh's Attributes (*Ithbāt*) which is the *Madhhab* of the *Salaf* in the issue, and then *ta'weel* or *tafweedh* of the meaning, which is the way of the Ash'arī speculative theologians. Imām an-Nawawī in his *Sharh* of Saheeh Muslim in particular made *tafweedh* of the *Sifāt Fi'liyyah* (such as *Nuzūl* [Descending], Joy, Anger, Laughter, Coming and the likes) and ascribes *ta'weel* to "a large body of the *Salaf*"[50] and then ascribes *tafweedh* to "the majority of the *Salaf*".[51] This indicates that there was confusion in regards to the issue with the Imām and that he viewed the *Madhhab* of the *Salaf* as fluctuating between *ta'weel* or *tafweedh*. Yet with this it cannot be said that Imām an-Nawawī was Ash'arī as he was a specialist in hadeeth and stayed away from *'Ilm ul-Kalām* agreeing with *Ahl us-Sunnah wa'l-Jama'ah* in many issues of *tawheed*, the issue of Allāh creating the actions of His creation, affirming

---

[48] Shaykh Mashhūr in his work *ar-Rudūd wa't-Ta'qqubāt* (ath-Thuqba, KSA: Dār ul-Hijrah, 1993), p.20 and 25.

[49] Mashhūr Hasan Āl Salmān, *ar-Rudūd wa't-Ta'aqqubāt* (ath-Thuqba, KSA: Dār ul-Hijrah, 1993), p.21

[50] Imām an-Nawawī, *Sharh Saheeh Muslim*, vol.6, pp.36-37

[51] Ibid. and vol.16, p.166

seeing Allāh on the Day of Judgement, the reality of īmān and that it increases, decreases and *istithnā'* is allowed in īmān,[52] the issue of one who commits a major sin, the Sahābah and other issues. Imām an-Nawawī also opposed Ash'arī dialectic in the issue of the 'first obligation' and defended the stance of the Salaf on the issue. Imām an-Nawawī stated in *al-Majmū'*:

As for the original obligation of Islām and what relates to beliefs then it is sufficient to have tasdeeq (affirmation) in all what Allāh's Messenger (ﷺ) came with and to believing in it with absolute affirmation without doubt. It is not compulsory for whoever achieves this belief to study the proofs of the Mutakallimeen, this is what is correct from the Salaf, fuqahā and the Muhaqqiqeen from the Mutakallimeen of our companions and others. For the Prophet (ﷺ) did not demand the likes of what we have mentioned from anyone. The same is the case for the Rightly Guided Caliphs, the companions and whoever came after them from the first generations. Rather, what is correct for the common people, and fuqahā (jurists) is to refrain

---

[52] *Istihnā'* in īmān is to exempt oneself from having complete and perfect īmān by stating "I'm a believer *inshā'Allāh*".

from delving into the details of kalām... rather it is upon them to restrict themselves to sufficing with absolute affirmation, and a large body of notables from our companions and others have indicated this. Our Imām ash-Shāfiʿī (ﷺ) has conveyed a severe prohibition (tahreem) of being occupied with ʿIlm ul-Kalām.[53]

Commenting on the hadīth, "*I have been ordered to fight the people until they testify that there is none worthy of worship except Allāh (alone) and until they believe in me and what I have brought...*", Imām an-Nawawī says in his *Sharh* of Saheeh Muslim (vol.1, pp.210-211):

In (the hadīth) is a clear evidence for the madhhab of the muhaqqiqeen (those verifying what is correct) and the majority amongst the Salaf and the Khalaf that when a person believes in the religion of Islām with a firm and resolute belief devoid of any doubt, that this is sufficient for him, and he is a believer amongst the Muhawahhideen. [And that] it is not obligatory upon him to learn the evidences of the theologians and knowing Allāh, the Exalted, through them. [This being] in opposition to those who made it obligatory and a condition for a person being from the people of the

---

[53] Imām an-Nawawī, *al-Majmūʿ*, vol.1, pp.24-25

Qiblah, [and who] claim that he does not have the ruling [applicable to] the Muslims except through this. This madhhab is the saying of many of the Mu'tazilah and some of our associates, the theologians (Mutakallimūn), and it is a manifest error...

The Mu'tazilah, Ash'arīs, Māturīdīs and the generality of *Mutakallimeen* hold that it is an obligation for each person to know the proofs for the existence of our Lord via rational and observable proofs. Some of them even go to the extent wherein they say that everyone should know the philosophical precepts which prove Allāh's Existence via *al-Jawhar wa'l-A'rād* (substance and accidents). With some *Mutakallimeen* even making *takfeer* of the one who died and did not undergo this inspection and inference (*Nadhr* and *Istidlāl*) in order to rationally prove Allāh's Existence. This basis was devised by the Mu'tazilah and then adopted by the Ash'arīs and Māturīdīs after them. Al-Qādī 'Abdul-Jabbār (d. 415 AH) stated in the introduction to his book *Sharh Usūl il-Khamsah*:

So he (al-Qādī 'Abdul-Jabbār) said: If a questioner asks: "What is the first (thing) that Allāh has made obligatory upon you", then respond: an-Nadhar (inspection, observation) that leads to knowledge of Allāh the Most High, because He, the Most High is not known by

THE 'AQĪDAH OF IMĀM AN-NAWAWĪ

necessity and nor by direction seeing, thus it is obligatory that we know Him through reflection and observation.

Then he stated on page 70:

When this is established then know that the intent by our saying that "an-Nadhar (inspection, observation) is the first obligation in the way to knowing Allāh", is that it is from those obligations that the mukallaf (the person bound by the Sharee'ah rulings) can never be separate himself from any angle whatsoever...[54]

The Ash'arī theologians held the same view, for Imām al-Juwaynī stated in *ash-Shāmil fī Usūl id-Deen* (p. 115):

Observation (an-Nadhar) and inference (al-istidlāl) that lead to acquaintance of Allāh, the Sublime, are two obligations...

And further on (p. 122):

...And if time passed by - from the time that religious obligations applied to him - in which he had the capacity for an-Nadhar (observation and deduction of

---

[54] Translation taken from Dr Abū Iyyād Amjad Rafeeq, accessed 19 March 2010: http://www.asharis.com/creed/articles/sipld-the-usool-of-the-ashariyyah-are-the-usool-of-the-mutazilah-part-2---regarding-the-first-obligation-upon-a-person.cfm

proof, rationally) leading to knowledge, and he did not inspect, despite there being no preventive barriers and he passed away after the time in which this was possible for him - then he is put alongside the disbelievers...

Al-Juwaynī here says regarding the one who did not make observation and inference, despite having the capacity to do so before he died, is considered a disbeliever. This is one of the more excessive views amongst them, whereas the others simply emphasize that knowledge can only be perfected through *an-Nadhar* and *al-Istidlāl* and that the first obligation is to observe, or have the intent to observe (in order infer from it the fundamentals of faith, such as a Creator and so on) and they differ regarding the one who abandons it, with al-Juwaynī's view being the most excessive of the views. Ibn Hajr al-'Asqalānī ﷺ first makes mention of the positions of Ibn Fawrak and his followers, and also that of Abū Bakr al-Bāqilānī and Abū Ishāq al-Isfarā'īnī (all Ash'arīs - being students of Abu'l-Hasan al-Bāhilī, the student of Abū'l-Hasan al-Ash'arī) on this subject. Ibn Hajr stated in *Kitāb ut-Tawheed* of *Fath ul-Bārī*:

> I have mentioned in Kitāb ul-Īmān the one who turned away from all of this [i.e. the stance of al-Bāqilānī, Ibn Fawrak and al-Isfarā'īnī] from its very foundation and who held on to His, the Most High's saying "So set your Face towards the upright religion, Allāh's fitrah

(meaning Tawheed) to which He has made mankind to be inclined..." (ar-Rūm (30):30) and the hadīth, "Each child is born upon the fitrah (i.e. inclination to Allah's recognition and Tawheed)..." For indeed the apparent meaning of the verse and the hadīth is that knowledge (al-Ma'rifah) is already acquired on the basis of the fitrah, and that (a person's) departure from that is through what (subsequently) happens to a person, due to his (ﷺ), saying "...then his parents make him a Jew or a Christian..." Abū Ja'far as-Samnānī, one of the heads of the Ashā'irah, agreed with this saying: "Indeed this one of the issues of the Mu'tazilah that remained within the sayings of al-Ash'arī. Branching off from this is (to say) that the obligation upon every person is to have knowledge of Allāh through the evidences that point to Him, and that taqleed is not sufficient in this regard."

Therefore, the Ash'arīs are in agreement with the Mu'tazilah on the issue of an-Nadhar wa'l-Istidlāl - and their foundation (asl) in this regard is the one and the same, and some of them have extreme views in this

regard. The reason for this is that the Jahmiyyah and Mu'tazilah were the pioneers of the proof called *"Hudūth ul-Ajsām"*.[55]

Shaykh Mashhūr in his book *ar-Rudūd wa't-Ta'aqqubāt* notes that the reason therefore for the confusion wherein some have linked him to the Ash'arīs is that Imām an-Nawawī agrees with some of their *ta'weel* when he transmits from their works yet agrees with the *Salaf* in many issues of creed due to his occupation with transmitted reports and staying away from *'Ilm ul-Kalām* and its details.

Furthermore, as many scholars and researchers have highlighted Imām an-Nawawī ﷺ lived from 631-676 AH which was the height of Ash'arī popularity and its speculative theology was becoming more established in the Muslim world, especially in the Levant and Egypt. Had Imām an-Nawawī lived longer then some scholars have noted that he would have clearly adopted the correct Salafī approach to creed as did his student Ibn 'Attār who witnessed the influence of Imāms Ibn Taymiyyah (661-728 AH) and adh-Dhahabī (673-748). Ibn Taymiyyah stated:

Almost all of the later scholars had some mistakes in their writings due to the misconceptions and confusions spread by the heretics. That is why one will find in many of the writings on legal theory, creed, fiqh,

---

[55] Refer to Appendix II

asceticism, Qur'ānic commentary, and hadīth, that a person will quote a number of different views and people but the view with which Allāh sent His Messenger will not be mentioned. This is not because they do not like what the Prophet (ﷺ) taught, but simply because they had no knowledge of it.[56]

Our Shaykh, Mashhūr Hasan, states in regards to these words from Ibn Taymiyyah: "**This totally applies to Imām Abū Zakariyyā an-Nawawī ﷺ.**"[57] It should also be emphasised that not every error in creed renders one a heretic or innovator for there is a difference between an innovation and an innovator, just as not all who commit *kufr* are rendered as *kuffār*. Ibn Taymiyyah stated:

It is not necessarily the case that all who make errors in creed are destined to be destroyed and from the losers. It may be the case that he made an errant ijtihād and Allāh will forgive him. It may also be the case that he did not receive all the information about that particular topic for it to be said that the proof is established against him.[58]

---

[56] Ibn Taymiyyah, *Sharh Hadīth un-Nuzūl*, p.118
[57] Shaykh Mashhūr, *ar-Rudūd wa't-Ta'aqqubāt*, p.29
[58] Ibn Taymiyyah, *Majmū' al-Fatāwā*, vol.3, p.179

One who calls to the Sunnah may fall into error in some matters and these errors are to be avoided yet the scholar is still upon good, one of the vile approaches in modern times has been the phenomenon of branding scholars who have served the Sunnah, such as Imām an-Nawawī, as heretics and innovators whose works should thus be burnt! This act of 'book-burning' the works of Imām an-Nawawī was the approach of the *Haddādī* sect[59] which is an extremist sect which brands the scholars of *Ahl us-Sunnah* as innovators and deviants. Imām Muhammad bin Sālih al-'Uthaymeen ﷺ stated in regards to Imāms Ibn Hajar and an-Nawawī:

> The two Shaykhs and preservers of the religion have their place of prominence, honesty and great benefit for the Muslim nation. Even if they made some mistake in reinterpreting some of the texts mentioning the Attributes [of Allāh], such mistakes are covered and immersed by what they had of virtue and great benefit. We suspect that what they stated was only the result of their own personal ijtihād and a permissible form of interpretation – at least in their view.[60]

---

[59] Named after its founder Mahmūd Haddād.
[60] Shaykh Muhammad bin Sālih al-'Uthaymeen, *Kitāb ul-'Ilm*, p.198

Appendix II: Aristotle's Influence on Speculative Theology

The original proof of *"Hudūth ul-Ajsām"*, as devised by Jahm bin Safwān (ex. 128H), made use of some of the basic notions which the atheist philosophers of that time were familiar with. Aristotle's Categories[61] laid

---

[61] Aristotle's Categories is a text from Aristotle's *Organon* that enumerates all the possible kinds of thing which can be the subject or the predicate of a proposition. The Categories places every object of human apprehension under one of ten categories (known to medieval writers as the *praedicamenta*). They are intended to enumerate everything which can be expressed without composition or structure, thus anything which can be either the subject or the predicate of a proposition. The ten categories, or classes, are:

Substance (*ousia*, "essence" or "substance"). Substance is defined as that which neither can be predicated of anything nor be said to be in anything. Hence, this particular man or that particular tree are substances. Later in the text, Aristotle calls these particulars "primary substances", to distinguish them from secondary substances, which are universals and can be predicated. Hence, Socrates is a primary substance, while man is a secondary substance. Man is predicated of Socrates, and therefore all that is predicated of man is predicated of Socrates.

Quantity (*poson*, "how much"). This is the extension of an object, and may be either discrete or continuous. Further, its parts may or may not have relative positions to each other. All medieval discussions about the nature of the continuum, of the infinite and the infinitely divisible, are a long footnote to this text. It is of great importance in the development of mathematical ideas in the medieval and late Scholastic period.

Quality (*poion*, "of what kind or quality"). This is a determination which characterizes the nature of an object.

Relation (*pros ti*, "toward something"). This is the way in which one object may be related to another.

Place (*pou*, "where"). Position in relation to the surrounding environment.

Time (*pote*, "when"). Position in relation to the course of events.

the foundations of this knowledge, and in Arabic they became known as *al-Maqūlāt al-Ashar* [The Ten Categories]. The metaphysics of the speculative theologians was preceded by Aristotle's metaphysics, and generally this knowledge was concerned with "bodies" (*ajsām, jawāhir*) and their "incidental attributes" (*a'rād*), or more formally "accidents". Here are Aristotle's ten categories, the first deals with "what something is":

1. Substance (*Jawhar*)

The rest are incidental attributes (*a'rād*) which deal with "how it is":

2. Quantity (*al-kam*) - dimensions and measurable features, length, breadth, width and so on

---

Position (*keisthai*, "to lie"). The examples Aristotle gives indicate that he meant a condition of rest resulting from an action: 'Lying', 'sitting'. Thus position may be taken as the end point for the corresponding action. The term is, however, frequently taken to mean the relative position of the parts of an object (usually a living object), given that the position of the parts is inseparable from the state of rest implied.

State (*echein*, "to have"). The examples Aristotle gives indicate that he meant a condition of rest resulting from an affection (i.e. being acted on): 'shod', 'armed'. The term is, however, frequently taken to mean the determination arising from the physical accoutrements of an object: one's shoes, one's arms, etc. Traditionally, this category is also called a habitus (from Latin habere, "to have").

Action (*poiein*, "to make" or "to do"). The production of change in some other object.

Affection (*paschein*, "to suffer" or "to undergo"). The reception of change from some other object. It is also known as passivity. It is clear from the examples Aristotle gave for action and for affection that action is to affection as the active voice is to the passive. Thus for action he gave the example, 'to lance', 'to cauterize'; for affection, 'to be lanced', 'to be cauterized.' The term is frequently misinterpreted to refer only or mainly to some kind of emotion or passion.

3. Quality (*al-kayf*) - perceived characteristics, color, shape, and so on.

4. Relation (*al-idāfah*) - how a substance is in relation to others, above, below, right, left and so on.

5. Place (*al-ayn*) - where it is

6. Time (*matā*) answering "when?" - temporal characteristics of the substance

7. Position (*al-wad'*) - how a substance's parts are ordered in relation to each other

8. Action (*yaf'al*) acting - what a substance is doing

9. Affection (*yanfa'il*) a substance being acted upon

10. Having (*al-mulk*) - what the substance has on

The speculative theologians therefore, armed with the notion of *Hudūth ul-Ajsām*, attempted to "prove" Allāh's Existence to atheists philosophers and applied it to the Texts which were potentially problematic for them. This was in order to hoodwink the atheists, which is part and parcel of the one-upmanship that goes hand in hand with atheist philosophy. So for example, when Allāh says:

$$ ٱلرَّحۡمَٰنُ عَلَى ٱلۡعَرۡشِ ٱسۡتَوَىٰ $$

"*ar-Rahmān* rose above (*Istiwā*) the Throne" {TāHā (20): 5}

Then the *Mutakallimūn* applied, as Dr Abū Iyyād Amjad Rafeeq, a Salafī creedal researcher from the UK, superbly parodied:

Hey, that's *al-ayn* (place) and *al-idāfah* (relative position) - and those are properties of *ajsām* (bodies) - this is *Jismiyyah* - and this opposes our proof of "*Hudūth ul-Ajsām*". Pull out the *ta'weel* gun, load it with a *ta'weel* (bullet) of Jahm bin Safwān, or Bishr al-Marīsī or any of the *Jahmī, Mu'tazilī* brands, 'zap', and you've got your end result. You've abolished that apparent *kufr* and *shirk* which necessitates Allāh is a body (thanks Aristotle, pseudo-Sabeans, Jahm, and al-Ja'd for helping us to understand the true *Tawheed*) and depending upon what bullet you used you've ended up with:

- ar-Rahmān conquered the Throne
- It's the Throne that made *istiwa* in actuality
- The Throne is simply Allāh's dominion and *al-istiwa* is an act that takes place therein

And thus those '*evil wahabis*', on the one hand, and those 'nasty, evil' philosophers are kept in check - all with a single 'zap' - this is powerful stuff. And look what we've found here:

وَكَلَّمَ ٱللَّهُ مُوسَىٰ تَكْلِيمًا

⟪And Allāh spoke to Moses (wa kallamAllāhu Mūsā), direct (Nisā 4:164)⟫

Hey, that's an <u>action</u> (what a substance is doing), its a temporal characteristic (an instance of speech that takes place and ends) which is an event (*hādithah*), and it also includes <u>quality</u> (*al-kayf*) because speech necessitates sound - something perceived with the senses, thus necessitating a "howness" - and all of this is pure *Jismiyyah* - *kufr* and *shirk*.

We know the routine now. Load, point, 'zap' and we can now have:

- Allāh created speech in the tree and the tree spoke
- Allāh spoke to Moses with his "eternal *Kalām*" that resides within His Self
- Allāh inspired the meaning into the heart of Moses

And if the *ta'weel* gun is not effective, just utilize a bit of *tahreef* instead and that way we can have:

- "And Moses spoke to Allāh (*wa kallamAllāha Mūsā*), direct" so its Moosā who actually spoke and not Allāh.

And thus those 'evil *wahabi mujassims*', on the one hand, and those 'nasty, evil' atheist philosophers are kept in

check, once again and we've dealt with them with a single stone.[62]

Dr Abū Iyyād Amjad Rafeeq again superbly parodies the Ash'arī inability to bring forth any justification of their creedal views via referral to the Salaf of the early generations:

> But just don't venture too close to the third century and before, because that's very a dangerous time and territory. Keep safe by keeping away from that zone, it won't be very friendly for you and some poor guys were getting executed, others imprisoned, and others beaten with sandals for indulging in this "*Kalām*" and making "*ta'weel*" " of the texts. So the rule is "Know your territory, play safe, and remain safe".
>
> If you've got a choice of a few hundred statements from the early *Salaf* on the issue of Allāh being above the Throne, with His Essence, don't go there, flee from it – it's dangerous, unfriendly territory. Stick with quotes from the later times. One quote from the later times can be just as

---

[62] See: http://www.asharis.com/creed/articles/iowfm-top-tips-to-become-a-better-ashari-2nd-tip---know-your-aristotelian-metaphysics-inside-out.cfm

effective as a full round of *ta'weel* bullets. So be wise and don't be wasteful in any way.[63]

---

[63] Ibid.

Jamiah Media Publications

Previous Publications:

1. *Before Nicea*. By AbdurRahman Bowes and AbdulHaq al-Ashanti (2005)
2. *Who's in for Iraq?* By Shaykh Abdul'Azeez bin Rayyis ar-Rayyis (2007)
3. *The Impact of Man-Made Laws in the Ruling of an Abode as Being One of Kufr or Islam*. By Shaykh Khalid al-Anbari.(2006)
4. *A Warning Against Extremism*. By Shaykh Salih Aali Shaykh (2008)
5. *A Critical Study of the Multiple Identities and Disguises of 'al-Muhajiroun'.* By Abu Ameenah AbdurRahman as-Salaf and AbdulHaq al-Ashanti (2009).

Forthcoming Publications:

1. *Shirk According to the 4 Madhhabs*. By Shaykh, Dr Muhammad al-Khumayyis.
2. *The Noble Women Scholars of Hadīth*. By Shaykh Mashhur Hasan Al Salman.
3. *The Madhhab of Ahl ul-Hadith in Fiqh*. By Shaykh Mashhur Hasan Al Salman
4. *Guidance on the Ruling on Giving the Khutbah in a Non-Arabic Language*. By Abu Najeed Isam bin Ahmad Saleem bin Mami al-Makki

Forward your orders to: admin@salafimanhaj.com or Darussalam, 226 High Street, Walthamstow, London, E17 7JH, UK. Tel: 020 8520 2666. www.dar-us-salam.co.uk